BUSINESS GROWTH DO'S
AND ABSOLUTE DON'TS

Business Growth Do's and Absolute Don'ts

Applied Wisdom from My Work with Dell, Costco, Amazon, and Multiple Start-ups

Carolyn Byron Lowe

LIONCREST
PUBLISHING

BUSINESS GROWTH DO'S AND ABSOLUTE DON'TS
Applied Wisdom from My Work with Dell, Costco,
Amazon, and Multiple Start-ups

ISBN   978-1-5445-2245-6 *Hardcover*
      978-1-5445-2244-9 *Paperback*
      978-1-5445-2246-3 *Ebook*

I dedicate this book to every founder, inventor, and entrepreneur who has ever doubted themselves.

I truly hope my twenty years of successes and failures help you.

Contents

Acknowledgments

For those who know me, you know I'm a talker, not a writer. I can run a mean spreadsheet, but ask me to write a chapter or a story, and it won't happen.

This book would never have made it out of my head without the amazing team at Scribe. I'm eternally grateful to Ronnie Lipton, my Scribe. I already miss our two-hour Friday sessions writing this book together over my mouthfuls of morning tacos. And to Jericho Westendorf, my Publishing Manager, for matching me with the perfect Scribe and keeping me on track.

All the things in my head and my experiences would never have been possible without some amazing people I've met throughout my professional career: Michael Dell, one of the smartest yet most humble leaders. Every amazing boss at

Dell, Inc. who I learned from who made me a better person and a better business mind. I can't believe that, twenty years later, I'm still in Austin after relocating from Boston for what I thought would be a "short-term" gig at Dell.

And finally, to my family. My husband, Ward, who didn't bat an eye when I told him I was writing a book, and my children, Alex and Fiona, who are why I do what I do. And finally, to my late mother, Leontine, who will never get to read this book but inspired all the drive and everything else good in me. (All the bad in me is my own doing.)

Introduction

"Should I keep going with my business or shut it down?"

When Kevin first showed up to my digital marketing agency, he was understandably frustrated. He had wasted the entire previous year and tens of thousands of dollars on two agencies that didn't know what they were doing. Neither of them could get him even close to profitability or his first million dollars.

Although Kevin was passionate about his high-end car accessory brand, poor sales persuaded him that people wouldn't buy it. "Is it even worth it?" he wondered. He started questioning the value of what he had built.

But nothing was wrong with his five-star product or its ability to attract an audience. What he needed to question instead was the competence of the agencies he'd hired to do the work. Our audit showed exactly why the product wasn't selling: They didn't target the right audiences. They had followed a misguided strategy, setting up his targeting all wrong and failing to optimize his ads to drive revenue. They'd created multiple campaigns and weren't spending nearly enough on any one of them to do any good.

They wasted his time, squandered his cash, and almost destroyed his will to continue.

When Kevin and I met, he was gun-shy and losing money. Spending $4,000 a month on advertising to make $3,000 in the same period, he was frustrated enough to close his business. But my agency had helped a good friend of his make millions of dollars, so he decided to try us as his last resort.

During our audit of his brand, we uncovered a second problem: when people complained in comments on his Facebook and Instagram ads that his car accessory was too expensive, Kevin had been defensive with them.

We coached him to see the comments not as adversarial but as an opportunity to emphasize quality, listen instead of argue, and respond with empathy.

Although it's hard to measure the impact of that transformation on sales, you can be sure it makes a difference. No one who disputes their customers can expect to scale.

Here's what's *easy* to measure: We repaired Kevin's broken strategy and made his advertising profitable in just four weeks. For only twice what he had been spending, he's now seeing a profit that's sixteen times that amount.

Since his business has taken off, Kevin has something to scale. In fact, the ads we did for him got so much attention that he not only proved the validity of his product and made money for the first time, but he also attracted a major auto manufacturer who wants to set up a partnership deal.

WHERE YOU COME IN

You probably have a lot in common with Kevin. You founded a company born out of your passion. You've poured good money into bad places, so you're nowhere near where you want to be. You know there are a million ways to spend money on a business, and it could fold up and die if you choose the wrong ones.

You've tried many, many things, but you just can't figure out what it takes to move the needle. I can tell you that trying doesn't mean you're doing it right. In fact, if I told you how many new clients have told us, "I've tried Facebook and

Instagram ads, and they don't work," you might not believe me, unless you've had the same discouraging experience.

I can also tell you this: if you think Facebook and Instagram don't work, then you—or more likely, your agency—have not done those ads in the right way.

Businesses are a lot of work, unknowns are scary, and you don't even know what you don't know, so you're probably frustrated and doubting yourself. Without a seasoned advisory board, the journey can be lonely. You're watching everybody else make millions of dollars online, and you can't figure out where you're going wrong. You need someone to tell you what to do.

And that's where this book comes in.

YOUR SOLUTION IS HERE

In the pages that follow, I'll show you what you can do on your own to grow your business. You'll learn how to optimize the most crucial areas of your operation. You'll learn the answer to key questions, such as:

- Why does connecting with my customer matter so much?
- How can I see a return on my spending?
- What can I do now to boost my revenue?

- What can I ask my team and my agency to get us on the right track to scale?
- Should I sell on Amazon or shouldn't I?
- How can I get out of my own way?

Plus, the one question asked by every single frustrated person who ever walked into our office:

- Can I be doing better?

And even this one:

- Should I close my doors?

This book will help you whether you've been selling online and got stuck at one revenue level or you fled to online sales after brick-and-mortar retail took an unprecedented hit in 2020. Either way, you'll understand how to spend your limited resources wisely and sell online profitably, so you can finally stop fearing selling online and actually *scale*. If you haven't reached your first million, you'll find that getting to that point can open up a lot of doors for you. Suddenly, you'll be able to attract funding, take on resources, and hire people so you don't have to do everything yourself.

HOW I KNOW WHAT YOU NEED

I began working in direct marketing and catalog marketing for technology companies in 1995. Four years later, when consumers were buying their first computers, Dell recruited me to help run their consumer direct-marketing division that sent out 200 million print catalogs a year. How different from today's online world that was! With direct marketing, you could be wrong 99 percent of the time—only 1 percent of recipients had to buy a computer—and you would still see a profit.

We certainly did, and it felt good to help Michael Dell make a lot of money. That upward trend continued. After two years, I moved to Dell's consumer eCommerce division, where I found even greater growth potential. We had no training or playbook for online selling at the time, so we just figured things out as we went along. Within two more years, we went from small, scrappy, and unknown—number five in the market behind Gateway—to number one.

Once we got there, however, the work wasn't nearly as much fun. I missed the exciting days when the brand was still emerging. I had been at Dell for six years when I left to recapture that excitement and my passion.

After having children and doing some consulting, I went to work on the online portion of a then-tiny consumer brand providing natural products for moms and their babies. My salary was half of what I'd made at Dell, but I so believed in the brand and the CEO's love for her mission that I happily worked even longer hours.

In three years, first as an employee, then as an agency, I helped that brand quadruple its revenue, moving from seven figures to eight, with more than half of that growth coming from Amazon sales. In fact, the business became so attractive that it was acquired by a multibillion-dollar international company.

I knew I wanted to do the same for other businesses. I began helping startups and other emerging brands. These were companies with limited means, which meant that any wrong move they made could cost them their entire business.

To help these companies in need, I co-founded ROI Swift, a digital marketing agency in Austin, Texas, in 2015. Since then, I've worked with hundreds of companies that have faced issues like Kevin's, both at his company's size and much larger. We focus on consumer brands with $3 million to $50 million in revenue—too small to be able to afford an expensive consultant like an MIT data scientist or a Facebook alumni with ten years of experience to guide them.

Many companies need this expertise, so by founding the company, I had found my mission and my goal: to help one thousand emerging consumer brands by 2030. After five years in business, we're heading to two hundred, and we don't accept more than thirty new clients a year at this point. That means it's unlikely that we'll take on eight hundred more in less than ten years.

That's also where this book comes in. I wrote it to help you and at least 799 other CEOs to avoid typical mistakes I've seen companies make. If you take away one thing from this book that helps your business—and you're likely to take away a lot more—I'll consider it a success.

WHAT YOU CAN EXPECT

This book is organized in two parts. In Part 1, you'll find valuable information about four business fundamentals that can have an enormous impact on your bottom line. Without them, it's not only difficult to scale but often impossible to sustain the scale or even the business. The first four chapters will show you how to:

- Start discovering and solidifying your *Core Values* as soon as you can.
- Apply them to *Hiring* people who support those values and *Firing* those who don't, for everyone's sake.
- Get *Customer Service* so absolutely right that it becomes *Customer Advocacy*.
- Learn the key business metrics—*Profitability*—and why it's essential to know yours.

These early chapters make up the foundation of a successful business. In Part 2, we'll discuss whether you should sell on Amazon or only direct-to-consumer (from your website with a platform like Shopify or BigCommerce) and what you need to know to crush both.

You may be tempted to skip Part 1 and go directly to Part 2 to tap into the potential goldmine of online sales. But I don't recommend it. One way or another, the people who skip the fundamentals of what makes a business successful often end up having to come back to them later—when it's a lot harder.

WHO DESPERATELY NEEDS THIS ADVICE, AND WHO CAN'T USE IT

This book is not for business-to-business brands. It isn't about generating leads. It's not for huge companies, either. (If Nike came to me for help, I'd turn them down.) And it's not for traditional retail companies that limit their sales to their brick-and-mortar. Nor is the book for brands that sell only in big-box stores, because I can't help them as much as I can help companies that have a direct relationship with their customers. What's more, the book is geared solely to for-profit companies, not nonprofit organizations.

If you're a founder, a CEO, or a CMO of an emerging for-profit consumer brand who is looking to sell online or increase your online sales, though, this book is definitely for you. I focus on emerging brands because I believe the world deserves choice—not just Coke and Pepsi. I want to help you bring that choice and your passion to the world. The book is also for you if you're pivoting or branching out to online from a brick-and-mortar store that had healthy sales until the COVID pandemic.

I wrote this book to support you in your quest to make informed choices to get your business not just to the next level but several levels up. It'll help you speed past the major areas that are holding you back. You'll finally get the right answers to the pressing questions about strategy, profitability, and the overall future of your company—questions many businesses struggle with.

In my twenty-year career, I've seen companies of all sizes make decisions of all kinds, from good to blatantly bad and costly ones. I've also seen them avoid making a decision altogether due to fear of making a mistake. In every chapter of this book, I'll help to steer you toward decisions that will grow your business.

Your first task on your business-scaling journey is to figure out what differentiates your business and where it's going, so that's where we begin.

PART 1

Nailing Down the Basics

When people go into business, as you would expect, they tend to focus on profits, and that's as it should be. A company that doesn't make a profit on a regular basis can't stay in business. The thing is, though, there are many factors to achieving success, including profits. The following four chapters lay them out.

CHAPTER 1

Scaling Core Values and Mission

If you were to order a $70,000 diamond ring, how would you feel about the company that sold it if the CEO boarded a plane to hand-deliver it to you at your front door? One large and successful company did that very thing because the action adhered to the brand's long-standing core values.

That level of commitment demonstrates that the company has nailed their culture and how they continue to be successful. They understand the importance of setting, practicing, and embracing core values that are authentic. The company asked to remain anonymous, and the incident was not made public, so you know it was no publicity stunt. The gesture was simply a pure reflection of what the company stands for.

I heard that story around the time I was at Dell and set up the partnership deal to sell computers through Costco, a brand that understands the power of living their core values. Everything I learned about that warehouse brand impressed me.

From their start, Costco has known that if they get four things right, they'll always make their stockholders happy. Those things—their driving principles—are to:

- Obey the law
- Take care of our members
- Take care of our employees
- Respect our suppliers

As an example of just how much they take care of their employees, when I worked with them more than fifteen years ago, their starting salary for a cashier was $46,000 with full benefits, almost $4,000 more than the average household income of $42,209 everywhere else at the time (according to US Census data).

They also promote from within rather than recruiting from outside: You can't get into executive management without having worked in a warehouse, so everybody in that company has lived and breathed those same values. And being promoted to management is not their ticket out of the warehouse stores. The CEO and management team visits the stores—not to look over employees' shoulders but to connect with shoppers and watch them interacting in the store environment.

By the way, the stockholders probably *are* happy. When I was fourteen years old, I won $10,000 by correctly answering a question in a radio station's contest. Many times over the years since then, I've wished I had put that money into Costco stock. When I worked with the company in the early 2000s, the stock was trading at $40 a share; last time I checked, it had climbed to almost ten times that amount.

Your company doesn't have to be Costco, or anything like it, to benefit from following their attitude toward customers and delighting them.

CORE CONCEPTS

You really can't be in business—or in business long—without identifying your core values and mission. Most companies, and probably yours, tend to know their mission even before they launch. The mission is their purpose, the problem they exist to solve or the customer need they exist to fill. For example, our company has always known our mission *and* our passion: to help emerging brands solve the problem of amplifying their voice in a noisy world. But it wasn't until we all sat down and talked about it that we figured out that we also had a clear vision.

Let's look at some additional definitions. I define an *emerging brand* by its revenue size: $50 million or less. So, not the Nikes of the world. We won't work with huge companies because it's emerging brands that really need us, and it's our mission to help them.

Out of that mission came our long-term *goal*, which, as you saw in the Introduction, is to help one thousand emerging brands grow by 2030. That's our destination, and the full staff is aligned with it. Alignment to both goal and mission matters because everyone in a company is on the same ship, and they can't feel aligned if they don't know where the ship is going. Using another analogy, all troops need to be marching in the same direction.

Give your mission and goal as narrow a focus as you can because if you try to do everything, you'll do nothing well and you'll end up working on stuff that sucks time and money but doesn't benefit the business. I witnessed another great example of a narrow and unifying focus in the early 2000s when I worked at Dell, which was so far down in consumer market share that Gateway, a company that's now out of business, was ahead of us. So everyone in the consumer division united in charging toward the goal of becoming number one.

Core values also support your mission. They are the principles that your entire organization lives and scales by. Not having them for too long could be why your company dies or at least stalls. Core values represent what you, the founder, care about, and they help to define your company's *culture*, which is the overall atmosphere inside the company.

Culture is what guides how people in the company treat each other and whether they align with your core values. If you care only about profits, you can expect a cutthroat type of culture. On the other hand, let's say that you care about treating customers well, as you should, so maybe that's one of your core values. If someone then makes a decision that is not in the interest of the customer, they're showing that they not only don't align with the core value but also no longer fit the culture.

For example, Apple's core value of simplicity extends both to products that are easy to operate and a limited product line.

The success of Apple, Costco, and other companies that understand the importance of authentic core values is the answer to the question I commonly get from new clients: "Why the heck do I need to worry about core values?"

Another way to express that answer is this: getting unstuck enough to scale is best begun by figuring out who you are, why you're in business, how your business is different, and what matters most to you. You might end up scaling anyway, but maybe not as much as you could. And it's a lot more time-sucking and expensive to figure out this stuff when you're big.

On the other hand, you don't need to know all of your core values at the start of your business. As I said, mission comes first. If you had asked me to name my core values when I started my agency, I couldn't have done it. They can be tough to find in the beginning when you're more focused on your mission. So keep an eye open for your core values as you go, and consider them a work in progress.

Don't wait as long as I did to identify them, though, or down the road, their absence will come back to bite you. I didn't even think about core values until about four years into my business—too late to keep me from hiring a lot of the wrong people and slowing our growth. The right time to think about them is within your first year in business.

HOW TO FIND YOUR CORE VALUES

Start by asking yourself where you want to go as a company. The next logical question follows: who's going to get you there?

Sometimes, as soon as you start thinking about these questions, an answer instantly and clearly emerges: "This is what I value, so *these* are our values." So you write them down and dictate their use to the organization. There's a risk to that method, though, because dictated values are less likely to achieve universal belief and buy-in.

To support buy-in, I recommend a collaborative method. It might sound like the question of the chicken and the egg, but one way to start to identify your values is to survey the people you've already hired in the context of where *they* want to go as a company. What are they excited about? What brings them joy in their work? If they were to win a million dollars tomorrow, what would motivate them to still go to work? What's their purpose?

Also survey yourself and your top managers about whether you and they would rehire the same employees. Then consider what experience has taught you about the qualities you look for in hiring staff.

TURNING BEST STAFF TRAITS INTO CORE VALUES

To illustrate how you can derive values from what you most admire about your employees, let me introduce one of ours. When we hired him to manage Amazon for clients, he knew a little about Amazon, he had been packing boxes for FedEx, and he had a high-school education. What we liked about him was that in his spare time, he was teaching himself the SQL programming language; no one was paying him to do it.

His desire to learn on his own made us realize that being intellectually curious was really important to us. It might be to you too because business founders tend to find themselves in uncharted territory. It's not as though you're working at McDonald's, with only one prescribed way to make burgers. In *your* business, there's no playbook, so you want people around you who can just figure stuff out and help you evolve.

The core value inspired by that stellar employee is "Always be learning." To encourage that, we set aside $3,000 a year per employee to learn anything they want that's somehow related to their job or to the company. We won't pay for, say, scuba diving, but we do pay for more types of classes than you might expect. For example, with the pandemic shutting down a lot of conferences, we paid for rest-and-recharge items like spa days, camping equipment, and a home putting green.

WHAT STICKY NOTES REVEALED

That core value turned up organically before the autumn of 2019, when I, my leadership team, and our Entrepreneurship Operating System (EOS®) did an exercise to discover the rest of the values. On sticky notes, we wrote adjectives to describe qualities that made our top performers great and our other employees not so great.

Sticky notes support a brainstorming exercise to come up with core values.

When we put them up on the whiteboard, we saw patterns emerging. The main difference between our A players and everyone else was caring about their work, putting the customer first, and being energized by it. They have a personal mission that drives them. It's what would make them come back to work the day after winning a million dollars.

An A player looks like this: when Facebook went down on Thanksgiving 2018, one of our team members took it upon himself to work through the holiday to get our clients' ads back up so they wouldn't lose Black Friday business. Now *that's* caring, and that's the kind of person who will help you get to your next level.

The opposite attitude is also easy to spot.

We've had people with a clock-punching mentality who would regularly roll in to the office late and casually miss conference calls with clients because they just didn't care. If they were faced with the Thanksgiving incident, they'd think, "Hey, too bad. Not my problem; I'm not working today."

So, that part of the exercise revealed another of our core values: "Care about what you do."

Another of our core values is "Make it better." Here's an example of this one in action: Like most companies, we provide our clients with reports on their performance. We realized we were spending a lot of money on reporting that wasn't very good. So, one of our team members took it upon himself to "make it better" by evaluating an automated solution that cuts our reporting costs by 80 percent and improves the reports by 100 percent.

"Keep an open mind" is our fourth value, and no one exemplifies this one more than our marketplace team leader. In the past, each person on the team was responsible for every part of three accounts. Although things were getting done, there was room for improvement. When he asked every other team member what they like most and least about their job, as he regularly does, he found out there was a better way to structure the work.

It turned out that team members didn't equally love every task, so they suggested splitting into two teams: one would focus on making Amazon listings look great and the other would focus on advertising those listings on Amazon, and each person could choose the team they were most passionate about. Because their leader kept an open mind, he listened and restructured the team around their ideas, and boom! Happier people because everybody gets to do what they like.

THE CORE VALUES OF MY COMPANY, ROI SWIFT

- Always be learning.
- Care about what you do.
- Make it better.
- Keep an open mind.

One year into having nailed down our core values, I can tell you that we have the right people on the team. We don't have any more B or C players. During the onboarding process, I give a core-value overview to every new employee, so they know exactly who we are, where we're going, and what matters to us. As a result, we're fueled for growth, and I expect the company's revenue to triple in the next year.

WHAT TO DO IF YOU'RE NEW AT IT

If you're a brand-new startup and you haven't hired anyone yet, think about companies you've worked for and people you've worked with. What did you like about them? Write the answers on sticky notes or a board. Maybe it's that they were honest, or they always came up with a new way of doing things, or they never took no for an answer, or they wouldn't rest until they made the customer happy. There you have what you care about: core values of honesty or integrity, innovation, tenacity, and customer satisfaction.

For Kevin, who you met in the Introduction, the only other "employee" was his partner, so they could only survey themselves. For them, their mission—to make a high-quality product—turned into the only core value they had when they started. They might have phrased it as "Accept and ship no less than high quality." As the rest of the story demonstrated, he also needed to adopt a mentality and a corresponding value of caring for the customer.

What if you've never worked for anyone, so you don't have personal experience to draw on about what worked and what didn't work? You might be like Michael Dell, who dropped out of college to start his computer company.

A few years later, he just hired people to provide the things he didn't know how to do. For him, the lessons came later, and some of them came the hard way. That's how it would work for you too if you didn't have this book to guide you.

You can also benefit from outside help, as we continue to do. To help us identify our core values and to guide us in their continual implementation in ongoing decisions, we do quarterly sessions with that EOS coach I mentioned before.

KEY QUESTIONS TO TRIGGER CORE VALUE DISCOVERY

Arriving at core values that everyone can get behind starts with looking into your motivations for starting the company. These questions can help with that process:

- What drives you? What drove you to start the company, and what makes you keep going? If someone said to you, "I'll make you independently wealthy if you walk away from your business," would you do it? If you would turn it down, why would you? Getting at what drives you also gets at your core.
- What are the traits of the people you'll need to help you

realize your mission? What are the traits of your best employees?

- How is your company different? Why would customers choose to buy from you over anyone else? Express that difference in one sentence.

Tecovas, Inc., a consumer boots and apparel company founded in 2015, expressed its difference in its mission: "High-quality boots handmade for fair wages, sold at an honest price." The founder came up with that mission because the traditional retail way to buy boots involved at least a 100 percent markup. He wanted people to be able to buy direct from the maker and avoid paying the middleman. In that mission statement, the words "quality," "fair," and "honest" easily translate to values. The company's laser focus on its mission has allowed them to expand into wallets, belts, jeans, luggage, and more.

CORE-VALUE TRAITS TO AIM FOR (AND THOSE TO STEER CLEAR OF)

Just proclaiming core values doesn't mean they'll work for you. These qualities will best support a healthy culture and unlimited growth:

- Make them positive.
- Make them authentic.
- Make them shared.

- Keep them brief and memorable.
- *Have* them.

Let me explain.

MAKE THEM POSITIVE

For core values to galvanize employees, they should sound positive and inspiring, unlike something like "Win at all costs." One airline makes it tough to find their core values, yet when you do, you see they keep changing. They do tend to talk about respecting their employees, but their pilots are often going on strike. This is clearly the wrong approach.

In fact, a page on the company's publicly posted standards of business conduct tells staff what to do if they see a colleague or manager violating ethics or committing other unacceptable acts. It includes a question from an anonymous employee who suspects their manager is using company purchasing cards to buy electronics for personal use.

The standards section goes on for almost thirty pages. If you hire only honest people who align with your core values, you probably don't need thirty pages about business conduct on your website. And even if someone *were* to take the time to read all of that, they might have trouble putting their finger on what the company cares about.

A message comes through loud and clear, but it's the *wrong* message: the company doesn't trust their employees. That fact would be egregious even if the employees were the only ones affected. But when you have a lot of miserable people who don't want to be there, their dissatisfaction comes across to the customers.

As a company gets bigger, I realize it gets harder to make sure that every new hire aligns with your core values. That only means that you'll have to work harder to incorporate them because you can't afford not to.

I have only twelve employees at the moment. But even if and when the company grows to fifteen times that size, the people who are responsible for hiring will understand the core values so well that no matter how many levels of delegation are involved, they'll know to keep those values front and center.

MAKE THEM AUTHENTIC

The pages on that company's website also contain a lot of nebulous talk about acting with integrity and treating people with respect. As a former customer, I can point to hundreds of times where that company did not treat me with respect. I also find that tone ironic because every single time I've flown on one of that airline's planes, I've heard flight attendants complaining about their employer.

The company should not be surprised if unhappy employees turn out not to be trustworthy.

The story brings up, in reverse, the need to honor your core values. Plenty of companies promote great-sounding values that they never intended to live up to; they're no more than window-dressing. When that happens, nobody's fooled— not the customers and certainly not the employees. The company's actions tell the real story.

Core values should not be the realm of the public-relations department. Those that only pay lip service might be worse than those with no core values at all because the lack of alignment between the written word and the company's behavior always shows to the employees and customers alike.

By contrast, authentic core values that align with behavior make a huge difference. Bigger companies than mine have the budget to pay my employees a lot more than I do. But my team members work with ROI Swift because they believe in my values and mission, and they know I believe in them, too. They align with them and feel fulfilled because they know they're part of something worthwhile.

As the Costco example showed, though, you don't need to be a small company like mine to have authentic values. Plenty of big companies do too. Another example, Entrepreneurs' Organization, a global network of thousands of founders of companies that earn more $1,000,000 per year, has established five clear values:

- Trust and respect
- Thirst for learning
- Boldly go!
- Make a mark
- Cool

Everything they do is around those values. For example, "thirst for learning" translates to valuable sessions presented by people like Mark Cuban and other highly successful entrepreneurs who are generous with their knowledge. And talk about cool: John Legend did a private live session for EO members during a recent global conference!

Core values that are not just for show but that reflect the essence of your company are key to putting your company on the right trajectory.

MAKE THEM SHARED

Core values reflect what a company rewards; they support its culture. When staff members sit around and say, "That's not my job," everyone loses. That includes the customers who don't reach their destinations sooner—or with all their belongings, as the following example from the same airline illustrates.

After customers complained about late departures, the airline promoted an initiative to be on time. Without unifying core values, though, it didn't turn out as planned. Pushing back from the gate on time meant they were leaving without people's baggage! Sure, they hit one metric—"Hey, we got 90 percent of our planes out on time!"—but you know customers were upset when their clothes didn't arrive with them.

By measuring everyone on on-time departure but not rewarding the whole team or uniting around a common mission, the airline unintentionally set up an internal competition. The pilots got rewarded only for the departure, so they took off no matter what. They had no incentive to help the baggage people, who took the hit when they didn't have time to load the bags.

If instead the airline had created a core value and a corresponding metric for overall customer happiness, that mess would never have happened. The environment would be collegial, not competitive, because everyone would be working toward the same goal—and customers would be less inclined to go elsewhere.

Similar infighting happens all the time in corporations with one team working toward an outcome that's at odds with the efforts of another department. That first team hits their bonus, the second one doesn't, and the customers usually suffer most of all. It doesn't have to be like that.

Contrast the behavior of that airline with one that gets it. Southwest works with its staff on core values that also benefit their audience, and on-time departures are one example.

The staff understands so well that it's everyone's responsibility that on three separate occasions, I've seen the pilot helping to load bags. Planes land, arriving passengers get off, departing ones get on—all with their baggage—and the plane takes off in the time it takes many other airlines to start boarding.

KEEP THEM BRIEF AND MEMORABLE

Limit your core values to three to five because employees are more likely to adhere to ones they can actually keep in mind. I've seen companies with ten core values. How many employees are going to remember them?

You can share a few meaningful core values much more easily, and everyone who's part of your company can feel good about getting behind them.

Follow up on a regular basis to make sure people do feel good. I recommend that you do an employee happiness score to make sure your values are working for your employees, which means they're working for your customers too. Core values support culture, and culture supports a healthy workplace that cares for employees and customers alike.

HAVE THEM

When I ask people in some companies that are much bigger than mine about their core values, they can't tell me what they are. If they don't know what's important to them, their employees won't either. But these are companies that have achieved some level of success because at some point, they showed growth. So you might well wonder how they did that—and how they are even alive—without knowing what they're about.

I suspect the answer is that while focusing exclusively on profits, they made decisions that have worked for a while, but will ultimately stunt further growth.

I'm thinking about one company with a culture that worked until it stopped working. Early on, the company enjoyed explosive growth. A lot of employees were motivated mainly by money, and they were willing to put in eighty hours a week only as long as the stock options were generous and they were getting rich. Without core values, though, that motivation disappeared as soon as the money and stock options dried up.

As I mentioned before, extensive hours at work is no accurate yardstick of productivity, but that company's flawed culture sure didn't get it. A manager writing up a performance review criticized an employee for leaving the building for lunch. You've got to figure that when someone can get dinged for going out to grab a sandwich and praised for being in their seat all day—even if they were just trolling the web, they're not going to put in their best effort. It was all about appearances; if you acted busy, you looked as though you were doing a great job.

This "appearances" company takes the classic "butts in seats" mentality that rewards their people not for getting the job done but for how many hours they sit at their desk. As a result, the company found itself full of people who care only about winning and getting promoted, not about the customer.

When the company went public, that attitude intensified, with everyone focused on dancing for Wall Street and putting short-term gains ahead of the needs of customers and employees alike. It didn't take long for many customers and employees to go elsewhere, and that ended up costing the company.

Even if the same company had had the technology at the time to allow staff to be able to work from home, you know their policy would not have allowed it. Even today, during a pandemic, they're requiring some office workers to go in because they don't trust them to work independently.

HOW TO APPLY CORE VALUES: FAVOR ACCOUNTABILITY AND TRUST

Once you've figured out what your core values are, you then need to apply them. Let those values guide all your decisions, including how and which people are hired and rewarded or fired. Shared core values will guide not only your staff's decisions but also their attitudes, like how they feel about coming to work, how much energy they put into their projects, and how they treat your customers.

When your employees align with your core values and you hold them accountable, you can trust your employees to do their jobs without needing you to micromanage them. Let them work where they want as long as they can get the job done. Some people are just more productive working away from their desk. Even outside of a pandemic, we don't schedule meetings on Fridays, so people can choose their workstations—home, a coffee shop, a park, wherever.

If I couldn't trust my employees to be productive in any environment—if I couldn't trust them with my car keys, my wallet, or my cell phone—it would mean I hired the wrong people.

Another signal that something's really wrong would be if I expected staff to work long hours on a regular basis. One of my best employees shows up every day at 9:30 and leaves at 4:30. He's motivated to be super-productive during those hours so he can be with his family all the rest of the time.

To further illustrate the relationship and value of accountability and trust, one of the metrics for our Amazon advertising team is to limit to one the weekly number of clients who are spending more than 15 percent of revenue on their ads. I don't care how they do it, only that they own the metric and get it done. That sense of ownership inspires innovation to get it done better and faster. And most importantly, they all have a weekly scorecard metric that they report on to the team each week.

Our weekly team meetings are another place to recognize and celebrate team members who apply core values. For example, we gave one employee a shoutout recently for "Always be learning" when he brought back great ideas about Amazon from groups he joined. We also recognized another team member for nailing "Care about what you do" with her relentless efforts to get one of our clients' advertising reinstated on Amazon after it shut it down for no reason. She worked through Amazon's many challenges until she succeeded.

During the quarterly meetings, in addition to reporting on

the financials, I further reinforce our core values. My slide presentation contains the photo and name of each team member and an example of a core value they demonstrated in the quarter.

The moral of these success stories is to hire, empower, and celebrate only people you trust. If you make them accountable by giving them metrics based on whatever you identify as the three most important aspects of their job, they can almost manage themselves.

A core value such as "We care about employees" will let you base decisions on a simple question—"Is this the right thing for our employees?"—and that will ensure a culture that fosters accountability and trust.

YOUR FOUNDATION FOR SUCCESS

The examples in this chapter have shown that core values have a stake in your ability to scale and why you need to figure them out sooner rather than later. Get them right, and do it before you get so big that your culture is already established for better or worse. It's so much harder and more painful to change a poor culture than to create a great one.

How far would you go to embody your company's core values? And how far would your employees go? If you and they would even consider chartering a plane to deliver a customer's purchase, congrats. You've created the foundation you need for success.

Do...

> ...have core values, and figure them out early on in your company.

> ...make sure they're clear to every employee.

> ...regularly reinforce them in all internal meetings.

Absolutely Don't...

> ...constantly change your core values.

> ...focus them on yourself rather than on your team and customers.

> ...have too many. Three to five is ideal.

WHAT'S NEXT

As you saw in this chapter, establishing meaningful core values can help you hire people who align with them. If you don't, you might end up with people who possess the right skills but don't fit in your company culture. In Chapter 2, you'll find out what else you need to know to craft the team you need to help you realize your goals.

Hire and Fire Based on Your Core Values

Ninety-nine percent of the problems facing many companies come down not to technology or to company strategy but to the wrong employees.

When it was time to fire my first team member, everyone in the company knew it. No one came right out and said, "Why is she still here?" But it was clear to all that this person was not performing or even trying to adjust to our culture. Her drama-filled life, negative personality, and bad attitude bled into the workplace and brought everyone down.

On top of that, this account manager turned out to not know much about her job, and she had no Facebook or Instagram experience. That could have been a temporary condition if she had made an effort to learn, but she hadn't. She spent almost all of her time complaining about our clients and just about everything else. Seriously, if she bought a smoothie on the way to work, she would find something wrong with it. She was exhausting to be around.

In time, clients started complaining about her, citing her ignorance and overall lack of courtesy. When they asked her for anything, it's not as though she failed to respond, but her tone was never calm or kind. They told me she acted as though she were doing them a big favor to reply at all, let alone actually say yes to something. She was much better at handing out excuses for not being able to fulfill their requests.

We would have been way better off training a junior-level person with the right personality for the job and with a commitment to (what became) our core values. I can teach someone all kinds of things, like running Facebook ads and making money on Amazon, but I can't change someone's fundamental personality, behavior, outlook, and values. I can't teach them to care.

These days, nine times out of ten, I'll take that junior person who fits our core values over a senior person who doesn't. Of course, some jobs require highly technical skills going in, but that's no reason to ignore culture fit.

You might be wondering why I even hired her in the first

place, and it's a great question. In my partial defense, though, we hadn't established our core values by the time she signed on, so we didn't know the right questions to ask. In fact, we were asking all the wrong ones. They were mostly limited to experience, and she had been an account manager at a big company. Even without core values, though, there's no denying that I overlooked an enormous red flag: in the interview, she bad-mouthed her previous client.

She had been with our company for nine months when we finally came up with our core values, which made us all too aware that she didn't share them. To paraphrase the book *Traction*, we had put the wrong person in the wrong seat, and we could no longer tiptoe around the elephant in the room: "Whoa, she's *never* going to work out."

When we used the "People Analyzer," a tool in the same book, to measure her (and every other employee) against our core values, we finally realized that this person wasn't learning and she didn't care about clients or about what she did or about making things better. To her, the job was clearly nothing more than a paycheck. She needed to leave *now*.

Although it was the absolute right decision to let her go, that didn't mean I relished the task. There was a lot of stress and anxiety leading into it because it's never easy to have that firing conversation. I didn't sleep at all the night before.

You know it's going to hurt when you take off the Band-Aid, so you need to just rip it off and get it over with. The very next day, we fired her.

BRIEF PANIC FOLLOWED BY A SIGH OF RELIEF

There was anxiety among staff after the termination. When anyone gets fired, it's typical for the remaining staff to fear for their own jobs. In this case, it was true even though team members were pretty sure why she stopped showing up. I assured everyone that the employee was fired only because she was a mismatch both to our culture and to her job. As I also told them, the employee's departure was definitely not a layoff. I let them know their jobs were safe, and the company remained healthy. Out of respect for the one I had fired, I didn't add what was also true: without that toxic personality running around, the company was even healthier than before.

Still, the benefit of firing that team member became clear to everyone soon enough. Her absence changed the workplace dynamic. It felt like the return of the sun after a hurricane.

This story illustrates that you can't be truly successful with the wrong people on the ship. Employees who are passionate about your values and mission—once you know what they are—and not only their paycheck will help you reach your goals.

I also came to learn that employees who are not passionate about your values are better off somewhere else. At least part of the reason the account manager lacked passion was that she didn't have the right temperament for the role. We found that out when we started asking each employee to take an Insights personality-profile test (less complex and more affordable than the better-known Myers-Briggs).

The brief online test shows which of four color categories each person falls into:

- Blue is precise and analytical—important qualities for roles in data science.
- Yellow is social, enthusiastic, and persuasive—like account managers.
- Green is caring and supportive—great for customer service.
- Red is competitive, strong-willed, and determined— often characterizing leaders.

We had placed a "red" person in a "yellow" role.

It was a totally wrong fit both for her and our customers, so no wonder she wasn't happy. If a person is going to spend forty hours a week at something, they *should* be happy. They should *not* dread going to work every day. There's a reason that Monday and Tuesday are the most active days for job searches on Indeed. After a great weekend, people are motivated to start looking for something to replace the job they hate.

Everyone deserves to be happy. By firing the dramatic employee, we were actually giving her a chance to be happy somewhere else rather than stay miserable with us. If you must feel and inflict short-term pain, consider it a necessary evil to achieve long-term gain. Of course, we—and, no doubt, she—would have preferred to know she didn't fit the role before she spent nine months in the wrong job and in the wrong culture.

The personality exercise also revealed another staff member who was in the wrong job. She was a behind-the-scenes computer wizard who, as it turned out, didn't love sitting at a computer all day, but she *loves* talking to clients. We moved her seamlessly into the account manager role because it aligns with her personality as much as she aligns with our core values.

Getting your core values right and hiring people based on them and your mission will ensure your ideal team. People can judge their own work based on how it aligns with those values. They know how their role fits into the big picture. They know that their work matters. Everything I've learned since that bad hire—how core values should inform hiring, the interview questions to ask, and how to interpret the answers—has meant I haven't had to fire anyone else who doesn't align with our core values *because they were never hired*.

Those are the lessons of this chapter. Before we move on, though, you should know this other reason to base every hiring decision on your core values: it costs a lot less.

At Dell, when we were faced with someone who didn't belong there, we would joke that we should show them the job openings at HP in the hope that they'd find another job and resign, because it's a lot cheaper than firing someone. When I fired the account manager, I saw just *how much* cheaper. My unemployment taxes went up by $20,000 a year!

Add the costs of clients you might have lost, or the time and money it might have taken to compensate for a lackluster performance, and you're talking money no small business can afford. It was still the right thing to do—she was a sort of cancer on the organization—but it would have been more right to avoid hiring the wrong person in the first place. I learned a valuable but expensive lesson.

VALUE-BASED HIRING FROM THE FIRST GLANCE

Put your core values up front even as you recruit. Make sure any successful candidate doesn't only have the technical skills or the willingness to learn them but also has the potential to pass this test: Will they be only a butt in a seat, there only to collect a paycheck? Or can they become so passionate about what you do that they would come to work even after winning that million-dollar lottery? They're the ones who will help you grow.

A small but growing company in Austin is a model of letting core values guide your hiring even at the initial point of contact. Sauceda Industries started as a T-shirt brand that couldn't find anyone to do fulfillment for them because they were too small, so they started a company to do that too. To begin with, their authentic, positive, brief, and memorable core values suggest why they continue to successfully scale.

VALUES FOR SMART HIRING

The core values at Sauceda Industries foster smart hiring:

- We say yes and...
- We shoot straight.
- We give a shit.
- We explore more.
- We build community.

Then, to encourage alignment throughout the company, these values are listed on their website's career page, right after this statement: "We look for people who are eager to solve problems and subscribe to five specific things we see as our core values." After the listing, they reinforce the message: "We live these values every day and want to work with folks who'd like to as well... If any of the above sound like a good fit for a person like yourself, take a look at our current openings below."

Perfect.

WHAT TO ASK AND HOW TO INTERPRET ANSWERS

One of the questions that has served us particularly well in interviews with potential hires is this: "If I were to ask your colleagues, clients, or boss to describe you in three words, which ones would they choose?" When I call their references, I also ask them to describe the applicant in three words. The answers tell us a lot.

Given our core values, we're looking for words like "inquisitive," "collaborative," "cooperative," "determined," and "innovative"—no matter what job opening we're aiming to fill. Of course, we're also open to other words. The adjectives used by who turned out to be one of our best employees were "honest, heartfelt, and positive." We're looking for parallels between the words we hear from the applicant and the reference.

Another telling interview question or prompt is "Tell me

about a time you made a mistake." We want people with a positive outlook who own their mistakes, rather than throw blame around (like our one-time account manager). Don't let an applicant's resume distract you from warning signs that they don't fit your company culture and values.

Follow up with, "What did you learn from that mistake?" They'd better have learned something, or history is likely to repeat itself. By even asking the question, you're also communicating that you understand that mistakes happen but expect lessons to come out of them.

REINFORCE CULTURE AFTER HIRING

When we hire people who've been the victims of a poor culture, it often takes them a while to relax into a whole different environment. For example, we hired someone in the past month who was afraid to ask for her birthday off because she had never been able to take it in her previous companies. She wouldn't even have dared to ask. She was blown away when everyone urged her, "Oh, definitely take the day off!" I was blown away for a different reason, "Are you kidding me? What kind of a company doesn't let you take a day off?!"

KEEP CHECKING, AND CHECKING IN

We use the analysis tools with everyone we interview,

but that's not the end of it. We continue to use them to ensure that our employees continue to display our core values and are excited about doing their job. Would they be more excited about doing a different job in the company?

I'll tell you what job I'm not excited about: invoices. I know how to do them, but I don't want to. There are other things I can be doing with that time that would have a bigger impact on the business. So I hired a bookkeeper who loves living in QuickBooks all day.

In fact, she said she can't believe she gets paid to do it. That's what you want: people with the right values and the right job.

We track each person's job performance with a weekly scorecard—another tool from *Traction,* but also something we did long before at Dell. In fact, every successful company I've ever worked at has a scorecard to keep everyone accountable to their job's metrics. For example, one of the receptionist's metrics is to answer every call within two rings. For sales-development reps, it's the number of sales opportunities created.

We hired a sales development rep who, it turned out, really wanted to be an account manager. He wasn't meeting the minimum requirements of the job, as specified on his scorecard, because he disliked making cold calls at all, let alone hundreds of them. So he wasn't making enough of them, and those he made, he wasn't following up on. By the time potential clients come to us, they're unhappy with their former agency and they want to move fast. If you don't get back to them within two days, they're gone.

I asked him point blank on our weekly call, "Do you want to do this job?" He said, "If I'm being honest, I really don't." The rep aligned with our values but not with the only job we had available for him. We would have moved him if we could. And because this revelation came up right after COVID hit, we laid him off so he could collect unemployment insurance, instead of terminating him.

We also learned from that hiring error: now applicants for that job take a sales assessment that's specific to our requirements and helps us find the people who love making phone calls. A little positive reinforcement doesn't hurt either. The leadership coach who visits us every quarter gave us these stickers to put on the sales rep's phone: "Pick me up. I make you money" and "Time kills all deals."

I've told you about two incidents in which using tools based on our mission and core values have identified people who shouldn't be in their job or in the company at all. Far more often, of course, those tools reinforce that we have the right team in place to go where we want to be.

Once you've nailed down your core values, apply them to your team and make sure your team applies them. Then make sure every team member is not only in the right job, but also loves it, your company, your mission, and your values. If they're not and they don't, rip off the Band-Aid for everyone's sake. You'll make them happy in the long run, including the person you let go, and you'll be setting up your business for success—because you really can't afford not to.

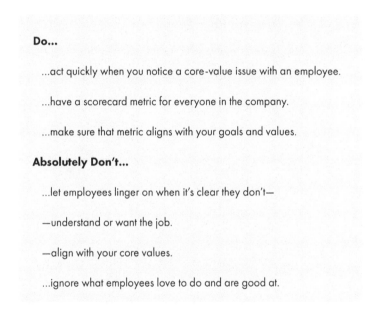

Do...

...act quickly when you notice a core-value issue with an employee.

...have a scorecard metric for everyone in the company.

...make sure that metric aligns with your goals and values.

Absolutely Don't...

...let employees linger on when it's clear they don't—

—understand or want the job.

—align with your core values.

...ignore what employees love to do and are good at.

WHAT'S NEXT

You've thought about your core values and you've made sure that everybody in your organization is aligned with them and is excited about their work. Now it's time to look outside the company and focus on your customers.

CHAPTER 3

Connection Turns Customers into Advocates

You know your company has a problem when your employees are embarrassed to tell anyone where they work. I was that employee, but it wasn't always that way. My former employer started out making great products and giving great customer service. Working there had been a source of pride for me.

As the years went on, though, the company made some key decisions that favored the bottom line over customers. Like many companies at the time, they moved the customer-service operation to overseas call centers staffed by people who lacked the knowledge and the helpful attitude of the

US crews. More often than not, customers were upset, and they were vocal about it.

Not only was I no longer proud to say where I worked, but I would actually hide the fact. When I got on a plane, I would keep my laptop closed so my neighbors wouldn't see the company logo on my PowerPoint deck and lay into me about the awful "support." I didn't even get a break at holiday gatherings, where some of my relatives would complain nonstop about the brand's transgressions.

The company put financial savings ahead of customers because they failed to calculate the impact and its likely price. They didn't realize that, although it might cost them less for each phone call, the savings disappeared when each problem was likely to require three calls. When business clients started complaining, though, the company—after a year—finally acted. They moved the business division back to the US, but the less-profitable consumer division stayed put.

You might think the company also lost the business of unhappy customers to competitors, but at the time, everyone else had gone offshore. They got away with under-serving their consumers until a competitor showed up with customer service as excellent as its product.

CUSTOMER SERVICE IS ALSO COMPANY SERVICE

Companies that put customers first almost always succeed. Those that fail to respect their clients tend to just keep treading water. Any decision that ignores the customer eventually hurts the company. Why? It's as simple as this: if you have no customers, *you have no business.* That might also sound obvious, but if it were, all companies would treat their customers like cherished guests.

No matter what kind of emerging brand you've established, customer service is probably more worth your best effort than any other single aspect of your business. Some companies prove they understand that. Years ago, I managed the quarterly catalogs for a Boston-based company that sold physical products. The Dingley Press, which printed those catalogs, formed one of my first and strongest impressions of what customer service should look like.

I traveled to Maine, Dingley's headquarters, to check the colors and resolution of the catalogs during their printing runs, often in the middle of the night. The company knew that nobody wants to go to Maine to check a catalog, especially in the dead of winter. So they did everything they could to make clients comfortable.

They provided accommodations in a homey apartment, which was cheaper than a hotel, but I can tell you it was also nicer for clients. And as soon as I walked in the door of both the apartment and the plant, a sign with this value statement greeted me: "If we don't take care of our customers, someone else will."

Those weren't just empty words. The company meant them. They were hyper-aware of bigger printers who could afford to offer better prices, so they knew they needed to focus on quality and customer service. They were courteous, friendly, and on time; they anticipated my every need before I even knew I had it.

MORE EXAMPLES OF STELLAR CUSTOMER SERVICE

I can't help but cite Costco again because of how well they get customer service. They showed that they put customers' safety ahead of revenue when the CEO insisted that they stop selling trampolines, despite their popularity. He said, "I don't think they're safe, and I don't want that for our members."

Rackspace Technology, a cloud-based host, also makes sure they get customer service right by, for one thing, making sure every tech support call gets picked up by the fourth ring.

As an emerging brand, of course, you would find it even tougher to replace lost revenue if you drop a product, but you do have a few advantages over huge established companies. For one thing, in a smaller company, you'd be closer to the product selection, so your company wouldn't have bought a potentially unsafe product to begin with.

The greater advantage is this: not having millions of customers means you can take your time and be intentional about creating a customer experience that feels like a warm and personal interaction. Consumers, especially younger ones, want to feel *connected* with the brands they support.

How can you connect with your customers? Show sincere appreciation for them.

The CEO of a high-end brand I've worked with sends a handwritten note to every person who buys something from them. That's what I call brand nirvana because it turns customers into advocates to their friends, on social media, and everywhere else.

And check out how Chewy.com connects with their customers. According to their website, the mission of the pet-products brand is "To be the most trusted and convenient online destination for pet parents (and partners), everywhere." When customers call in, they can expect to be engaged in a conversation about their pet. After that, the company not only knows the pet's favorite food but their *birthday* as well. If the company contacts the customer because they haven't ordered in a while, and they find out it's because the pet passed away, they'll even send a sympathy card.

That's taking things to a whole other level: customers aren't just buying dog food from this company, they're entering into a relationship with people who communicate that they care about them and their pets.

When you put the customer first, you take it upon yourself to figure out what the customer wants and then you give it to them. "A" for the course is to go all the way to what would delight the customer. At the very least, thank customers for their first purchase. This can be in the form of a text or an email, and it may or may not have your picture on it or a story about the brand, but it definitely needs your name, not the company's.

The note doesn't have to be handwritten—a set-it-and-forget-it automated email works just fine. The important thing is that it doesn't feel like automation and that it does tend to establish a connection. A lot of my emerging-brand clients have received personal responses to those emails on the order of, "Thank you so much for taking the time to write to me. It means so much that you've reached out. I love your brand."

CUSTOMER SERVICE VS. CUSTOMER *CONNECTION*

Few companies take customer service more seriously than Amazon, and you could do a lot worse than emulate them. Amazon bases their treatment of their audience on "customer trust," one of their founding principles. In fact, their insistence on putting the customer first can be rough on their sellers. If someone who orders something on Amazon says the package didn't arrive, they're always going to believe the customer, not the seller who swears they sent it.

Customer trust is also why Amazon has cracked down on people who leave fake product reviews. The company has removed millions of them because the attitude is that as soon as the customer doesn't trust the content, Amazon has lost them.

Amazon reflects outstanding customer service. They start with what the customer wants and work backward from there. For example, when they found out the one thing that makes people happy is super-fast delivery, they started competing with even themselves to get it done. When two days wasn't fast enough, they got it there on the same day, and now it's two hours, where possible.

But customer service is not the same thing as customer connection. Unlike Chewy.com, Amazon—and Wayfair, by the way—doesn't actually *connect* with the customer. The relationship is purely transactional.

At this point in the chapter, you probably won't be surprised by my statement that providing outstanding customer service is mandatory. Consider it the bare minimum because it alone might not be enough. As long as Amazon is basically unsurpassed in their field, that's everything they need to do. But if a competitor were to show up that shares or even exceeds Amazon's differentiators *and* they go out of their way to connect with their customers, that could change the equation.

As the example in Chapter 1 suggests, Southwest Airlines nails both customer service *and* connection. I'll give you a personal example: I didn't join their rewards program, and I've spent only about a few thousand dollars on their flights. I'm Joe Schmo to them. Yet they treat me better than the airline with which I've flown more than a million and a half miles since 1999 and I have elite status for life.

On Southwest, though, if I can't make a flight I've booked, I can apply its price to another flight. They don't believe in penalizing customers—no change fees. When my dad was sick in Boston, and I was flying back and forth on Southwest from Austin, often needing to cancel at the last minute, the airline made it easy and earned my loyalty.

LISTEN TO YOUR CUSTOMERS

Your company is not Southwest, Costco, or Amazon, but

like them, you need to take customer service seriously because it seriously affects your revenue now and in the future. The best practice for both providing excellent customer service and encouraging connection is to hear from customers themselves what they're thinking.

At Dell, we had a customer advocacy group that would invite about twenty customers at a time to visit headquarters and give product feedback. After listening to them, we would use what they told us to shape the product. Those were the pre-web days; today, of course, it's so much easier to get feedback and to get it more often.

There's no substitute for checking in regularly to make sure your customers are happy. If they're not, change things until they are. You'll get that valuable opportunity because you asked them and listened to what they had to say.

Here's still another useful way to listen to customers: at one company where I worked, we would offer customers the experience of participating in a select group of product testers. The message was "Hey, we're thinking about bringing this product to market. Would you like to try it for free and tell us what you think?" People loved being a part of that, and of course, we loved the result. Not only did they feel a deeper sense of partnership with us, but they also saved us the expense of releasing some products that were unlikely to succeed.

And you'd better listen when people are unhappy or even bored. It's not too late to rescue a drifting customer until they stop talking to you, said the then-COO of NPD Group, a global market research company. "If your customers are complaining, you haven't lost them yet. You have a chance to convert them to happiness." I couldn't agree more.

A great way to find out if they're unhappy or bored is to check customers' buying frequency. Take the example of a men's high-quality custom-clothing maker that hired me as a consultant. Their shirts fit because their tailor made house or office calls to measure customers. Despite that level of personal service, the shirts' prices were still half the price of retail because the company didn't have to carry inventory.

But some customers were buying from them only once over a period in which it was typical for other customers to reorder. So first we sent out an email: "Hey, I notice you've bought only one shirt from us. What did we do wrong?"

Here's why those customers never came back: on shirts made by the company's former vendor, buttons would fall off after the first washing.

ACT ON WHAT YOU HEAR
The company found a new factory and eliminated the qual-

ity problems, but the one-time customers didn't know it. The situation presented a great opportunity for a customer "win-back" campaign. It was so worth doing because it's so much easier and cheaper to keep the customers you have than to acquire new ones.

So I made a friendly phone call to each one-time buyer who responded to my Google drive sign-up request for a twenty-minute slot. I engaged them further about their experience with the shirts, then I told them about the quality improvement and offered, "We'd love for you to come back. Can we send you a free shirt?"

ENGAGE AND RANK

What about you? How often do you get on the phone with your customers? In the early days of his company, Michael Dell would regularly answer customer calls. That's a really smart way to find out what's on people's minds and show overall value of your customers. No one can make good decisions if they're sitting in a tower removed from their customers. You have to know how what you're proposing will affect them.

If you can't talk to people individually, survey them every six months. Make sure you include this simple question:

"On a scale from one to ten, with ten being most likely, how likely are you to recommend us to a friend?" That question gets at the Net Promoter Score (NPS), one of the numbers you need to know about your business. (You'll find more about this and other essential numbers in the following chapter.) People who rate you a nine or ten are your promoters—they love you. Scores of seven and eight come from neutral/passives. People who give you a six or below are detractors, and it's worth your time to find out why they're not raving fans and what you can do about it.

Also ask "What's working?" and "What's not working?" When my company ran an eCommerce store for a client, a survey told us that what wasn't working was the website. I got on the phone and the website with them and located exactly where they ran into user errors that we could help them avoid. At the same time, I was taking advantage of the opportunity to find out more about them. I was *connecting* with them.

THE DANGER OF NOT ENGAGING

On the other hand, if you don't want to talk to customers or you see them as only dollar signs, you're missing out on the opportunity to learn about and connect with them. You're also throwing away precious access to your most valuable source of feedback about your product. Both of those lost opportunities will affect your bottom line sooner or later.

Not enough companies realize this. In fact, some think

of customers as a necessary evil, rather than the treasure they are. I've heard things like, "Oh! I've got this horrible customer who..." Plenty of companies don't listen to their customers, and some that do know to listen don't act on the feedback. I'm thinking of one client whose customers kept telling them that the product needed improvement. Until the company fixed it, they lost 20 percent of their market share.

You might also feel like some companies that fear and hide negative comments on social media. What they don't understand is that negative comments are really a gift. They offer an opportunity to show that you're listening and that you're willing to respond with genuine empathy and thanks for reviews of all kinds. If they're bringing up a valid point, take it to heart and work with it. The only comments you should hide are those from bots, trolls who have obviously not tried the product, and nasty people in general.

SHOW YOUR LOVE

Now that you've seen how poor customer service can negatively impact your growth and your bottom line, ask yourself how you can deliver great customer service, open a dialogue with customers, and connect with them. If you're selling online, consider your customers to be a goldmine—one of your most valuable assets. Consider every interaction with any of them to be an opportunity to learn something and to make things better. And train every employee to behave that way every time.

Figure out and practice the best ways to show your love, and you can be sure they'll love you back.

When I was no longer proud to say I worked with the company that had stopped valuing their customers and were downgrading their customer service, I knew it was time to leave—even if that mistreatment didn't affect the bottom line. But it usually does.

Do...

...make customers a priority as a core value.

...find an authentic way to connect with your customers.

...make them raving fans by connecting your purpose with what matters to them.

Absolutely Don't...

...ignore your customers.

...choose revenue over customer satisfaction.

...knowingly make a decision that will negatively impact your customers.

WHAT'S NEXT

Building on what you've learned so far about core values,

hiring and firing, and customer connection, it's time to turn to the fun stuff. Chapter 4 is about how to make money and directly grow your business.

CHAPTER 4

How to Be Profitable

A company that makes natural deodorant and body-care products came to our agency for help with running Facebook and Instagram ads. We started, as we always do, by asking these crucial questions:

- What's the value of your average order?
- How often is each customer repurchasing?

They didn't know the answers. *Seriously?* Well, how about this one?

- What's your customer's lifetime value?

They didn't know that one, either. They had been in business three or four years by then, yet they didn't know their basic business numbers. So they didn't know how much they could spend to acquire each new customer, which is kind of horrifying.

It's not as though they had been failing. They had been doing okay, with a few million dollars in revenue. They had found a lot of success through word-of-mouth by bloggers in the natural products space. They were also doing okay with their ads, spending a couple thousand a month.

But because the natural-product space is a finite universe, that amount was about a third of what they needed to spend to be able to scale revenue. They needed to go more mass-market and compete not just with products like Tom's of Maine, but also with ones like Dove and Secret—whose customers don't read blogs about natural products.

As long as the brand didn't know their numbers, they had been slowing their growth by thinking short term and not investing enough in their customers.

When I explained, the client was stunned. The first thing they wanted to know was, "How can we find them?" As I told them, "The data is all in front of you; it's *knowable*." It's all sitting in the eCommerce database.

I went in and pulled their numbers, including their average transaction value and average time to repurchase. Their customers normally spend $25 each time, and the product lasts about ninety days, so that's about $100 a year in orders per customer. That meant they could spend up to $20 to acquire each customer, and anything less than that would amount to greater profit.

They were spending $2,000 a month, which translated to $10 to $12 in customer acquisition cost. With a monthly spend that small (both in this case and in general), Facebook has a hard time finding enough people to serve up the ads to. It takes input to be able to generate output, and with $2,000 a month, the platforms don't have enough data to work with.

Doing some back-of-the-envelope math based on those numbers, I could tell them how much they needed to spend each month to gain enough volume to lower the cost of acquiring each customer.

We ran Facebook and Instagram ads for them that tripled their monthly spend—thus giving Facebook enough to work with—and got the amount to acquire each customer down to $8. That means they were profitable on that very first transaction, not only on all future ones.

KNOW YOUR BUSINESS NUMBERS

Of course they would have been a lot more profitable if they had known their numbers a lot earlier in the life of their business.

Don't make their mistake. Know your numbers, so you can know whether you're profitable, and so you can scale. If you're a new brand, I understand that it's hard to know them.

But as I did with the deodorant brand, you can still guess-timate based on the price of your product and how often you can expect customers to buy from you.

You'll arrive at other numbers you need to know by finding out the numbers that make up your profitability equation, including those three main numbers: lifetime value (LTV), average order value (AOV), and average days to repurchase.

The first two numbers show you what you can pay to acquire customers. Knowing that third number—how often customers will purchase from you—helps you mine your relationships with your existing customers, rather than overlooking them as you chase new ones.

As the shirt story showed you, once you acquire a customer, you don't have to pay to acquire them again. In the case of the deodorant, the brand could spend more of their margin, or break even, on that first sale because they would make it up in the other sales in the same year. That fact suggests this: lifetime value and repurchase value matter more in the kinds of businesses that customers buy from more than once (as opposed to maybe a seller of private planes) or frequently (as opposed to during a pregnancy).

There's another reason you need to know your numbers: If you're going to raise money, potential investors demand them (as any *Shark Tank* viewer knows). They expect to know things like how you acquire customers, for how much, and whether the process is repeatable and sustainable.

	Company A	Company B
Average Order Value	$40	$80
Cost of Goods Sold and Expenses	40%	40%
Margin after COGS	$24	$48
Break-Even Cost per Acquisition	$24	$48

Knowing your average order value and your costs and expenses will show you how much you can profitably spend to acquire a customer.

REDUCE COSTS

Even if you don't know the big three numbers, I'm sure you know what you pay to produce and ship the product versus what you charge for it.

Of the many roads to profitability, a big one to look at is whether you can get the product cost down without reducing the quality or harming the customer experience in any way.

But to be profitable, you also should monitor what portion of that product cost goes to advertising and, again, what you spend to acquire each customer.

It might sound contradictory, but it can take spending more on advertising per month to spend less to acquire a customer. If you don't spend enough, you won't grow your customer base because the Facebook/Instagram algorithms would not be able to collect enough data to lower your cost per customer acquisition.

Getting the upfront cost right also means not having to keep spending to acquire the same customers because those customers are already there. Put them on a subscription plan, and you can sit back and watch the money roll in. (We'll talk more about this in Part 2.)

Of course, it's even more important not to spend too much. We've seen people who were spending more than the lifetime value of customers to acquire them. There's a fine line between spending enough to get the lowest cost per acquisition and spending so much that you've gotten all the customers who are cheaper to acquire, hitting a point of diminishing returns, so your cost starts going back up.

So *how much* should you be spending on Facebook? *What should your budget be?* Those are the big questions, and the answer is: Find the sweet spot of profitability. You need to get to fifty conversions ("add to cart," "view product," or best of all, "purchase") per week for the Facebook algorithm to optimize. You can scale up from there.

For example, let's say you're getting customers on Facebook for about $20 apiece, and you know Facebook needs fifty of those conversions a week for the algorithm to work, a total of $1,000 a week.

When you divide that total by seven days, you get $142.85. Then round it up to $150. That's what your daily budget needs to be just for "prospecting": acquiring new customers. Now add $30 to $50 a day for "retargeting": reengaging customers who've bought from you or went to your website but didn't purchase. That brings you to $6,000 you need to spend every month on Facebook to become profitable.

THE $40,000 OLIVE

My favorite story about getting costs down comes from American Airlines. As part of a massive cost-cutting initiative more than thirty-five years ago, they calculated that if they removed one olive from every salad served on the planes, nobody would notice and the airline would save no less than forty thousand dollars.

It worked—they saved, without customers ever missing the extra garnish. So far so good, but the airline didn't know where to stop. They started cutting corners in ways that noticeably and negatively affected customers. Those cut corners included charging even their frequent fliers for changing flights or booking an exit row and charging everyone else for bags.

TEST RAISING PRICES

Once you set your prices and customers accept them, it can be frightening to think about changing them at all, let alone actually raising them. But if you can overcome the fear that you'll lose customers enough to test raising prices, you might find you can do it. As soon as you do, of course, you'll also change your profitability equation.

How much do you need to make on each transaction? For example, let's say you sell sweaters and your average order is $50. Each sweater costs $10 to make and $5 to ship, a possible profit of $35 (not counting any overhead). Are you fine with spending $35 on advertising and breaking even on that first sale?

As you've seen in this chapter, the answer should come down to how often customers make repeat purchases. If the repeat sales don't support that much, the alternatives are spending less or charging more.

As an agency, we also faced the need to raise our prices

and felt trepidation around it. We had some legacy clients on an old flat-fee pricing model. For one particular client, that model had made sense before their account became far more complex. But they were paying the same amount, and we were barely breaking even. It was clearly time to overhaul our pricing system.

We studied how much time we spent on each client and who was profitable for us and who wasn't. When I identified the break-even clients, I was scared to approach them, but I knew I had to. I told them, "These are our new prices. They'll allow us to dedicate the time your account needs."

We weren't delivering an ultimatum, because I wanted to be sure we didn't lose any clients. Of course, not every client accepted our first proposal. In one instance, after going back and forth a few times, the client agreed on prices that were less than new clients pay but way more than they paid before. We also became aligned in incentives, meaning that the more revenue they made on ads, the more we made too. Then, after a few more years, we brought them up to the market value of our services.

MASTER THE CASH CONVERSION CYCLE

Optimizing ads for growing revenue, reducing costs, and raising prices aren't the only ways to be more profitable. Also think about how you can hold onto your cash longer.

Is there any way you can get paid sooner and pay your creditors later?

If at all possible, avoid being like an apparel brand we work with. I heard in October that they'd already paid for clothing that wouldn't be made until February, and they wouldn't be able to sell to their customers until March. They had to take lines of credit to do it.

Needing a lot of cash for inventory is a drawback faced by many consumer brands. Dell solved that problem efficiently (if not kindly) with their policy of holding no more than two days' worth of parts at any given time. They made many of their suppliers store their stock on one side of a fence in the warehouses. Dell would take it as they needed it—based on actual customer orders in hand—right before it went on the assembly line. They wouldn't actually pay for it until fifty days afterward. The company was getting paid before they had to pay for anything. That's almost a print-on-demand model.

It's hard for a consumer brand to know how much product to make when you don't know how much you'll sell. You don't want to have to pay for inventory you'll end up eating because it doesn't sell. That's why some brands prefer to "launch" by pre-order—taking orders for products that don't exist. That way, they can gauge interest in the product; pre-orders tell them how many to make or even whether to make it at all. If the pre-order offer generates little or no interest, the company has learned it without the expense of making more than a prototype.

There's really no downside to pre-orders. You build a website and make sure you can eventually manufacture the product, but you're not paying for it until you get the orders. Unlike going to investors, it doesn't require giving up a chunk of the company in exchange for needed cash.

Another smart way that small companies (and start-ups, in particular) test the waters without laying out their own cash is with a crowd-sourcing campaign on a site like Kickstarter, GoFundMe, or Indiegogo. It's smart because they test demand for the product and maybe gain feedback at the same time they raise manufacturing funds.

What's more, the people who invest—even for as little as $10 to $30—feel a sense of ownership that often translates into product loyalty.

Any company can benefit by maximizing its cash conversion cycle. We're a service agency, which means we don't have the overhead of a consumer brand; there are no products or manufacturing infrastructure. In our case, it's employees who make up our biggest cost by far—80 percent of it. So it was easy for us to figure out what to do, but that doesn't mean we figured it out as soon as we should have; it took us a year.

Here's where the cash-flow issue came in: We would invoice clients on the first of the month and give them thirty days to pay, but we were paying employees on the fifteenth and the thirtieth. We were having to pay the first half of our team's monthly salary before most clients paid us.

So we told clients that when we renewed their contracts, their terms would shift to fifteen days. No one objected, and now we keep more cash in our hands that we can use for reinvesting in employees.

CHECK YOUR PROFITABILITY

The point of this chapter was to get you thinking about your business in terms of its potential for profit and scale. Now that you've learned which business numbers you need to know, there's no reason not to know them. If you don't know them, I suggest you put this book down right now and go figure them out, because if you don't, you probably won't even *be* in business in five years, let alone scale. Then ask yourself what you can do differently to improve your cash flow and profitability.

Once the deodorant company knew their numbers, they could make much smarter decisions about where and how much to invest. With the right budget, we were able to double their profits from their direct-to-consumer online sales.

Do...

...learn important numbers, including average order value and product costs, to find your profitable customer acquisition cost.

...know your conversion cycle and look for ways to improve it.

...challenge your team to find ways to be more profitable.

Absolutely Don't...

...wait until years into your business to figure out the KPIs (Key Performance Indicators) that make your business healthy and scalable.

...fail to invest in acquiring new customers—especially if you have a high rate of repeat business—or your competitors will acquire them!

WHAT'S NEXT

With the fundamentals of core values, hiring and firing, customer service, and now profitability under your belt, you're ready for the second part of the book. Let's talk about how you can make money selling online. After a quick look at why online selling beats limiting yourself to brick-and-mortar retail, we'll start with direct-to-consumer.

Selling Online

You're reading this book because you're selling online now but not crushing it, or you're not yet selling online at all but you want to. Either way, you already know it's worth your time to figure out how to nail it. As we dive into the nuts and bolts of online selling in Part 2, you'll find out exactly how to do it.

Ever since online selling became a thing, it has always had huge advantages over brick-and-mortar retail. Take control, for example. With online, you have a greater ability to own your own destiny. In retail, on the other hand, you're at the mercy of the buyer. When I worked for the maternity brand, Walgreens yanked one of our products (because it wasn't performing and shelf space is finite), and it was really hard to make up that revenue. Yanked products can also happen on Amazon and any other online platforms that you don't own, but never because of lack of space. You never want to have all your eggs in a retail basket.

Lack of control also translates to not having a *voice*. You can't easily tell your brand's story or have a say in shelf placement as you can on eCommerce platforms, even on Amazon these days. And without the ability to tell your story, it's hard to create customer loyalty.

Another huge advantage of online sales—whether you're selling direct-to-consumer or you're selling to or through Amazon—is their lightning speed, as opposed to traditional retail, which takes f-o-r-e-v-e-r. I can put up a Facebook ad for a client today and make them $10,000. The other big online benefit is I'll know it right away; online sales show up in real time. And, if you're selling direct-to-consumer on an eCommerce platform like Shopify or your own website, you can see how many people are on your website—right now.

For example, I knew instantly that sales went crazy after one of my clients got a mention in the biggest online magazine in their industry, because I could watch it happen on my phone. Compare that with retail where you may have to wait up to a week for reports.

The next two chapters will help you nail your online selling.

CHAPTER 5

Direct to Consumer

Let me tell you about an emerging brand that started out great and got into trouble. A former beauty trend analyst in New York founded a company around her line of skincare products that sold well, primarily through storefront retailers.

At the beginning of the COVID-19 pandemic, though, her retail partners canceled orders. She would have lost a big chunk of her business if she hadn't wisely turned her focus to direct-to-consumer online sales.

She got two more things right: She developed a well-designed, quick-loading website, as anyone who sells direct-to-consumer must. She also leveraged her former publishing contacts and got her line featured in *Allure* and *Vogue* magazines.

But although that kind of coverage is undeniably great press, it's not sustainable. You can't count on being in a national magazine every month unless you're paying to be there.

Instead, she was counting on her Facebook advertising. But her digital ad agency at the time designed a campaign with poor structure, strategy, and targeting that got her less than a one Return On Ad Spend (ROAS, pronounced "RO-as"). *That* means that for every dollar she spent, she got less than a dollar back in revenue, so she lost money on every transaction. If she had continued in that direction, she would've had to raise money to stay afloat.

When I met her as part of a mentorship program, the brand was relatively new, so there wasn't much data on repurchase cycle or average order value. All I knew was that she needed to reach a two ROAS, and quickly. My agency took her on as a client, got her account right, and doubled her revenue for the same ad spend.

Getting her account right meant recasting her campaign based on the 40-40-20 success formula of advertising in general. It applies to online sales in particular:

- Forty percent is the *audience*: are you talking to the right people?
- Forty percent is the *product and offer*: is what you're putting in front of those people relevant to them?

- Twenty percent is the *creative*—the look (and maybe sound) of the ads: are they "thumb-stopping"—compelling enough to stop people in their tracks and speak to them as they scroll through their feed?

This story illustrates why creative counts less: Imagine ten people in a room, and two of them have a headache. If those two get an ugly Facebook ad that offers them two ibuprofen delivered on the spot for $2, they're going to jump on it—doesn't matter how bad it looks. But give those other eight people the same message, even beautifully designed, and nothing will happen *because they're not the right audience.*

Ninety percent of the time when we take over an account, the old agency was targeting the wrong audience with its Facebook ads. That was certainly the case for the beauty brand. Their customers are in the forty to fifty-five age bracket, but the ads were going to eighteen- to twenty-five-year-olds. No wonder they weren't profitable! The creative worked, though, so we didn't change it, only the people who saw it.

Product sales on the web beat retail for speed, profitability, and brand control. There are so many factors involved in selling online in general and direct-to-consumer in particular, and advertising is just one of them. But it's not where you need to start. To drive revenue on your direct-to-consumer online sales, do as the skincare guru did and think about how and where you should sell. That's what we're doing here, in this chapter.

WHERE TO SELL—DIRECT-TO-CONSUMER ALONE?

A good first step is to consider whether to limit your business to direct-to-consumer or add other channels. This brings up the big question on everyone's lips: "Do I need to sell on Amazon?" If you decide it makes sense to, you'll learn a lot about working with Amazon in the next chapter. But for now, here's what you need to know:

Limiting sales to your own website is the way to go for consumer brands whose products are not sold in brick-and-mortar retail. That way, you don't have to pay a middleman and you can own the whole experience, including the relationship with your customers, and you can better control your branding.

The moment you sell your product to a retail outlet—Target, Walmart, a grocery store chain—or even in one specialty coffee shop or bike store, it'll end up on Amazon whether you like it or not. The reseller will put you there. And in the next chapter, you'll learn how to make it pay if there's any way to.

The other consideration is the nature of your product: if it weighs more than three pounds and costs less than $15, it won't be profitable to sell on Amazon. Customers won't shell out more than the price of the product to ship it, and you won't want to bother if there's little left after Amazon gets their cut. On your own site, not only do you save the cut, but you can offer slightly slower but lower-cost shipping.

HOW TO SELL DIRECT-TO-CONSUMER

But that's not the first or even the most important thing you need to nail if you intend to sell direct at all. Before you spend a dime on advertising to drive traffic and sales, you need a good foundation—a website that can convert shoppers into buyers.

NEVER SEND GOOD TRAFFIC TO A BAD WEBSITE

When clients come to us to run their paid advertising, the first thing we do (well, after finding out if they know their numbers) is audit their website in Google Analytics. We look at three metrics, and if your website doesn't ace them, we won't take you on as a client. We won't be able to help you with a website like that, and you'll hate us. Instead, take the money you were going to spend on ads and go fix your website.

Three Key Metrics for Any Direct-to-Consumer Website

To get your website right, you've got to get these factors right:

Page-Load Time

Assume that every one of your potential customers has attention deficit disorder. If any page on your website makes them wait more than three seconds to load, don't even bother paying to send them there; 40 percent of them will abandon it. Use a free tool called Google Page Insights or GT Metrix to check load times, and get a developer to fix any page that takes too long. The main problems we usually see are big images or too many apps or code. Streamline and remove anything you're not using.

eCommerce Conversion Rate

If your price point is $100 or less, at least 6 percent of the total visitors to your website should add something to a cart, at least 4 percent should make it to checkout, and at least 2 percent should actually convert. If they don't, check your website and work on figuring out where they went astray. If your average order value is more than $100, shoppers tend to make multiple visits to your website before purchasing, so you will likely have less than a 2 percent conversion.

Metric	Benchmark
Add to Cart	6% or more of visitors
Checkout Started	4% or more of visitors
Purchase	2% or more of visitors

Shoot for these numbers to know that you're on the right track. If you're not, look into what needs to change.

For example, if they didn't fill the cart, maybe something confused them or the product details turned them off. If they didn't commit to checking out, maybe the shipping cost is too high.

Or maybe the site makes it take too long to navigate or check out. The holy grail is Amazon. They've got everything saved so customers can buy something in one click—in less time than it takes them to sneeze. That should be your goal for your site.

Mobile Experience

Make sure the experience for your mobile customer is as good as it is on the desktop, especially if mobile counts for a lot of your visitors. You can find out with two more useful bits of info from Google Analytics: how much of your traffic comes from mobile devices, and how your conversion rate on mobile compares with desktop.

For a jewelry brand that came to us, the desktop was converting at 6 percent, but the mobile, responsible for *70 percent* of their traffic, was converting at only 1 percent. The problem came down to a notice directing people to "click here for wholesale," which was no longer what the company did. Although the banner was tiny on the website, it took up the whole mobile page—a horrible customer experience. Again, the answer was to go to a developer, not to us, as we advised them.

Some software programs, including Hotjar and Mouseflow, let you monitor customers' online experience in real time, on both desktop and mobile devices. You can watch how and where people navigate, how long they spend in each place, and if and where they stop before checkout. That's valuable data because you'll know exactly what needs adjusting.

HOW TO GET MORE OUT OF YOUR ONLINE STORE

Along with testing the raising of prices, as the previous chapter suggested, here are two more ways to increase the value of each transaction.

Cross-Sell

This method involves putting together a virtual bundle to try to interest a customer in a second, related product. For example, let's say you're a clothing brand. When a customer looks at a shirt, you can give them a few options. Sure, they can buy it alone, which is great. But you really hope they'll jump on your offer to bundle that shirt with a pair of pants and get a discounted price for the whole outfit.

The types of cross-sells I *don't* recommend are those that require the customer to move back to a product page to choose a size or to read about the product. You never want to take someone out of the purchase path where they could change their mind about buying at all. Keep it simple so all they have to do is click "add to cart" to take advantage of the cross-sell.

You can set up bundling with simple plugins on your site. Many of our clients who are on Shopify use Bold Bundles, which eliminates the need for separate pages.

Up-Sell

The customer has made a choice and is ready to buy when the website shows a suggestion: "Hey, would you like to add on this great product?" For example, it's what happens when someone buys a computer, but they see that if they spend more, they can get a better monitor or more memory. That's an up-sell, intended to encourage your customers to impulse-buy more than they intended.

The easiest up-sell for you to offer and for the customer to accept is a multiple: you simply present a discount offer for a three-pack instead of the single item chosen.

WHERE TO FIND YOUR DIRECT-TO-CONSUMER CUSTOMERS

Get the web experience right, and only then are you ready to start talking about advertising and other ways of driving traffic to your website. Selling direct-to-consumer implies *having* consumers, so let's look at how, besides advertising, to reach them.

I sort sources of customers into two main categories: those you pay for on a recurring basis (including advertising) and those you don't. Even the "unpaid" ones have a cost, but it's generally less and one-time-only. Beyond that, one type of source can fit into either category. First, we'll look at that hybrid.

PAID OR UNPAID SOURCES

Endorsements and mentions by industry influencers—in magazines, blogs, videos, and websites—can be paid or unpaid, depending on how you get them. You'll hit the jackpot if an influencer finds out about you on their own, but of course, you can't rely on that. More typically, upping the chances of a worthwhile product mention takes money (hiring a PR agency, which can be expensive) or time (contacting influencers on your own), or both (some influencers you contact or who contact you will insist on pay-to-play).

As you learned about the skincare line at the start of this chapter, those plugs can't be your only strategy, but they're still great if you can get them. They live forever. Five years after one of our clients got a plug in a *People* magazine article, it was still generating sales for them. A feature in an Instagram post fades quickly, but even then, you can quote the plugs as a testimonial on your website.

Paid Sources

Our agency has taken brands to eight figures in revenue that do little advertising other than paid social and paid search. They can be tremendously lucrative if they fit your business and you do them right.

Paid Social

By paid social, I mean advertising on channels like Instagram, Facebook, Snapchat, and TikTok. It's probably the most effective way for your emerging brand to grow without having a pharmaceutical-company-size budget. For example, Facebook advertising alone took the boot company I mentioned earlier to $1 million a year run rate (sales)—roughly $85,000 a month—in online revenue in less than a year.

Paid social lets you target your offer and your audience far better than traditional "spray and pray" forms of advertising—TV, radio, billboards—ever could. Social channels allow you to learn about your audience while they're learning about you because they know a lot about the people who engage with them. That intelligence is there for your taking, and of course, you can use it to your advantage.

Let's say you've just come up with an innovative traveling water bowl for dogs. It's an emerging brand that nobody knows about, but you know dog lovers are already on social channels posting about their dogs. As they post, they reveal a lot about themselves, their dogs, and their preferences, and the channels are listening—collecting and sharing that data to help you target those owners and optimize your ad dollars.

The other great benefit of paid social is the ability to connect the praise of delighted customers with people who haven't tried your product but wonder whether it works. "Social proofing" can take one of two forms: 1) showing ads with a lot of likes and comments from happy customers to potential customers, or 2) using a testimonial from an industry publication. Either form is a slam-dunk because it provides credibility and the reassurance people are looking for.

As we've seen, you'd better target the right people in the right way or you'll waste your money and efforts. And, you've got to spend enough to make paid social get enough data to find the right people for your products.

For our clients, we typically spend 80 percent of their budget on finding new customers and the rest on re-engagement and retargeting for those already familiar with the brand. That adds up to a minimum of $200 a day on prospecting and retargeting/re-engagement.

Paid Search

As you know, those three results at the top of a Google or Bing search page don't get there by accident. Companies pay for that ranking because they know that consumers are more likely to click on the first links they see. They pay less for the few results below the top ones on that page. Some cost as little as 10 cents per click, and others can cost up to $50 per click.

The holy grail of ranking shows up below the paid-search results on the first page. These are the domains that no one has to pay to place; their ranking happens organically because they're so popular. It's really hard to get there, though, which is why many companies pay for the favored location.

Paid search refers to more than just "search," the most familiar type, which is most likely to fetch links on a page. In fact, it's on only one of four primary types of paid search, and you can be successful with them all for as little as $5,000 a month. The other three types are shopping, display, and videos.

When people see "shopping ads," for example, they see each featured product's picture, title, and number of stars. Paying for top ranking on a shopping search has led to great results for a lot of our clients' brands. On one of the major eCommerce platforms, it's simple to set up an automated product feed that you can use for shopping and for display ads.

In addition to product-specific display ads, there are also *generic* display ads. So, if a customer were to research a pair of boots on a website and go to another website that displays ads, Google would follow that customer around the web and keep serving up a display ad for the boots on other websites that display ads, like recipe websites. (Until the customer made the purchase or the brand's retargeting period expired, whichever came first).

That type of display for acquisition is known as "remarketing" or "retargeting" because it targets people who have been to the brand's website. The other type shows your display ads to people who have not been but are looking at travel sites in general.

Display ads attracted a lot of viewers to our client, a real estate developer who was selling condos. We targeted the ages, incomes, and geographic locations of likely buyers who received display ads that showed a picture of the condos and the option of seeing floor plans. While we paid only for people who clicked through the ad, a lot more people found out about these great new downtown condos.

Videos, the fourth main type of paid search, lets your video play at the start or in the middle of the video that the user clicked on to watch. The price varies based on whether people are forced to watch it or can skip it.

Buy Both

It's best to do paid search and paid social together, which admittedly adds to the cost but should more than pay for itself. They complement each other, as in this typical scenario: A customer sees your ad on Facebook but doesn't click through. The next time they do a Google search, if you bought that search term, your product will show up at the top of search results.

You might see multiple touch points and plenty of time before someone buys, particularly with a more expensive product. How long does it take a customer to purchase? It depends on the average order value (AOV). We see brands with $40 AOV receive over 80 percent of its purchases within the first forty-eight hours of customers' visits to the site. By contrast, a brand with an $800 AOV will attract less than 20 percent of purchases within the first fourteen days.

I wouldn't stop at that estimate, though. With Google Analytics, you can see the average time it takes your customer to purchase and the number of times they come to your website before they do. You can then use that data to know how long to follow around customers with your ads and search results.

For one brand with an average order value of $45, 85 percent of viewers would buy on the first day or not at all. You'd need a different strategy for an expensive product that people would have to give more thought to and might forget about. That's where your various channels working together come in: you need to be everywhere people are searching, which one channel alone can't do.

Affiliate Marketing

Here's how affiliate programs work: First, you put a cookie on your website to connect with a network of publishers and websites. A blogger who decides to feature you can link back to your website or Facebook page and receive a portion—typically 5 or 10 percent—of any sale generated within a predetermined period. That beats having to pay for only placement.

The bigger affiliate platforms like CJ Affiliate and Rakuten limit themselves to brands that have a million dollars in annual online revenue. If you're not yet in that bracket, you can work with ShareASale or eBay's Pepperjam Ascend. You can also explore influencer platforms, such as AspireIQ or Grin, some of which have curated millions of content creators. Those platforms do all the links, legal contracts, and campaign analytics. You just introduce your brand and the platform hooks you up with appropriate affiliates.

Whatever you do about affiliates, I recommend that you avoid coupon sites like RetailMeNot.

Customers who go there for a discount already know about your brand; they were going to buy anyway, so there's no point in paying them a percentage. I would rather put the money toward acquiring new customers.

Unpaid Sources

Along with paid sources, email marketing is where 90 percent of our customers' sales come from. I consider it an unpaid source because, although you pay for some email marketing services, you don't pay every time you email a customer.

Before I go any further, let me disclose that we're agency partners with an email program called Klaviyo. It happens to be my favorite one, and they're not paying me to say that. (Nor, by the way, is Google or Facebook paying me to mention them, although we're also agency partners of theirs.)

What I like about the Klaviyo program is that it lets you do more targeting of email addresses than more basic programs that only collect addresses in one big list. It also lets you segment—customize messages to particular audiences. A basic email program, like the ones from most eCommerce platforms, do have the advantage of being cheaper. But with email's potential to generate as much as 50 percent of your revenue, an extra $50 or $100 a month is worth it.

And because basic programs won't let you customize, every customer gets the same message, say, "Sign up now and get 10% off your first purchase!" With Klaviyo, on the other hand, which costs 15 or 20 percent more than a basic program, the customer's signup can set off an entire process of getting acquainted that drives sales.

For example, for a pet brand, dropdown menus on a segmenting program can encourage customers to provide the name and type of their pet. Oh, a parakeet named Fluffy? Then on the backend, the welcome email can mention Fluffy by name. If Fluffy's owner doesn't sign up on the spot, that lack of response triggers an email two days later showing happy parakeets and maybe a few stories or some education about them.

When someone makes a first purchase, a good email program lets you send out a personalized email from the CEO: "Thank you so much for your order. We started this company for people like you. You're why we love what we do. If you ever need anything, reach out to me by responding to this email." You know the customer feels better about a company like that than one with an anonymous message of "Your order just shipped, and here's your tracking number."

You can create that warm feeling with automation—set it and forget it, so you don't have to constantly send out campaigns. Automation also means that when someone buys a thirty-day supply of something and twenty-five days pass without a reorder, it's easy to send a reminder. "Do you need to buy some more? Here's a one-click way to do it." Or you can send an email to people who leave something in their cart without buying.

In every case, you can A/B test various ways to target them. A/B testing means trying different approaches to similar groups of customers and seeing which work best. You can test any number of things, including frequency, length, and timing (such as the number of hours after a cart is left filled). For the brand of one of my clients, I tested two subject lines for emails that went to people who deserted their carts. One was "Hey, you left your cart behind," but the one that worked was "What did I do wrong?" along with a sad emoji. That wasn't a surprise; a question typically draws a better email open rate than a sentence or phrase.

In this case, the question led to an open rate that was crazy high—more than 45 percent, compared to the typical 20 to 30 percent. Inside the email, "Wow. You left your cart and didn't finish your purchase. We feel so bad and want to know what we could have done better. Just hit reply. Unlike with big companies, when you do, you'll reach a live person from our company."

A lot of people actually did reply, telling us things like, "I just decided to buy it on Amazon," or "the promo code didn't work." Because we sent that email and got replies, we learned about some issues we could deal with: a customer-service team member could call the person and help to place the order over the phone, while the web team or developer could work out the promo-code bug.

Please note: The question-and-emoji approach won't work for every brand. You need to know what your customers will respond to. Fortunately, you've been listening to them ever since you read Chapter 3.

Size Schmize

People tend to be obsessed about the size of their subscriber list. Bigger is always better, right? Not necessarily. List size is all about vanity. What good is fifty-thousand addresses if their owners haven't opened any of your emails in the past six months?

I care about *engagement*, the sanity metric. It's the number of people who opened an email from you in the past sixty days. A strong open rate sends a strong message to the Gmails, Yahoos, and Outlooks of the world that you're a trusted brand. You'll have a better shot of that if you're not sending emails out to everyone. (Of course, you'll also be better off if your emails aren't getting stuck in spam folders; make sure they're not.)

In fact, when we set up a client with a new email platform, we spike the open rate by targeting only people who've opened one of the client's emails in the past thirty days.

We can juice it and the email providers' interest even more by inviting a reply to a request like, "Tell me what you're interested in."

Here's still another important way to support a healthy open rate. As you did with your website, preview your emails to make sure they look good on both desktops and mobile devices. I can't think of a platform that doesn't let you do that, and of course you can just check everything on your phone. We're still finding emails that were designed for desktops in an increasingly mobile-centric world.

PARTNERSHIPS

A great—free—way to build a customer base and sales revenue is to get together with a few brands and agree to work together. That work might take the form of promoting each other or exchanging emails lists. The key is finding brands that complement rather than compete with yours and that have similar customers. Successful partnerships I've seen include a footwear brand and an apparel company.

SUBSCRIPTIONS

If your product is consumable like coffee that gets purchased over and over, consider offering a subscription on your website or on an eCommerce platform like Shopify. (Amazon's Subscribe & Save was the likely inspiration for other platforms' subscription models.)

The beauty of subscription, of course, is that you can set up willing customers with a delivery every month or two in exchange for a 5 or 10 percent quantity discount. You don't have to keep after customers, and it's better than pre-orders because it constantly recurs—well, at least until the customer cancels. It's like free money.

On Shopify, subscriptions and auto-delivery are easy with apps such as Bold Subscriptions or ReCharge. You pay for the app but not for every subscription or every time it's fulfilled.

OWN YOUR CUSTOMER

In this chapter, you've learned that nothing beats direct-to-consumer sales for certain types of businesses. When customers buy directly from your website, you "own" them, their experience, and yours—as well as every dime of the sale. You've also learned strategies for finding those customers in the first place and then generating sales. That knowledge can translate to millions of dollars in revenue.

When retail fell apart on the skincare line, direct-to-consumer sales were a godsend but only when the advertising worked. The founder/CEO doubled her paid social results with the same products and same website, but better targeting. Her email marketing helped engage people who visited her website and didn't purchase, as well as provide continuing education on product use and more.

Do...

...audit your website on speed and conversion rates and the overall customer experience. Improve them if you need to.

...make sure that if you advertise on Facebook, Instagram, Snapchat, or TikTok, you spend enough to lower your customer acquisition costs.

...use email marketing to build your brand advocacy, create a relationship with your customers, and drive revenue.

Absolutely Don't...

...skimp on your email program. Testing, automation, and data are critical to your success.

...spend money on advertising until your website is optimized for speed and conversion.

WHAT'S NEXT

With these strategies in hand for setting up your website and choosing the best channels for selling direct-to-consumer, you're ready to learn about Amazon—the elephant in every online sales room.

CHAPTER 6

Selling—and Not Losing Your Shirt— on Amazon

When a natural-cleaning brand came to us two years ago, almost all their sales came through retail. Amazon was responsible for less than 1 percent of their sales while the rest of the industry was killing it there. Their national sales manager, who was in charge of working with the brand's Amazon channel, didn't know how to be profitable on it. We pointed out why they weren't making money on any of the products they sold there: most of their products were too heavy and inexpensive to sell individually and make a profit after paying Amazon's fees.

We cut or grouped (into multipacks) any of their Amazon

products that cost less than $15, leaving them with half of what they had been selling on the platform. They were able to raise the average order value to a profitable level, even counting the cost of Prime delivery. (No one's going to wait seven days for their kitchen-counter cleaner to arrive, but in the past, the company thought that was the fastest delivery they could afford.)

Two years later, the company's Amazon business has not only become profitable—it has grown to fifteen times its original size.

SHOULD I OR SHOULDN'T I?

At some point, all consumer brand owners who sell online (and even those who don't) ask themselves the burning question, "Should I sell on Amazon?" Here's the answer: certain brands should—and then, only strategically—and certain ones should not at all.

A lot of companies, lured by Amazon's enormous traffic, just jump in without knowing if it's right for them. Some lose so much money that they would have been better off doing nothing.

Unlike them, though, you'll go into that decision with your eyes open because you're reading this chapter.

You're about to walk through the economics of selling on Amazon—they're different from both retail and direct-to-consumer. Then you'll know whether Amazon is a channel you should embrace or flee from.

THE PROS AND CONS OF AMAZON: A LOVE/LOATHE RELATIONSHIP

When you bring up Amazon in a group of online sellers, people tend to get excited for a variety of reasons. Everyone has an opinion, based on the degree of success or failure they've found there. Let's look at Amazon's pros and cons compared with retail.

THE PROS

So many eyeballs: It's hard to resist a channel that customers flock to. With more than 2.4 billion combined desktop and mobile visits in September 2020, Amazon is by far the most visited eCommerce property, according to a study by Statista,[*] a company that tracks such data. Customers visit en masse because of massive selection, often-cheaper prices than those of competitors, ease of use (one-click ordering!), and speedy delivery.

With millions of people a day already on Amazon, they can discover your product without your having to pay to get

[*]   Source: statista.com/statistics/623566/web-visits-to-amazon.com

them there. You pay only for a percentage of sales, unless you buy pay-per-click ads on Amazon. Even then, it's worth it because you've got the potential buyers right where you need them.

No need to wait: Unlike brick-and-mortar retail outlets, which limit when they'll take on new products, you can launch something on Amazon at any time. You also don't have to wait to get paid. Amazon typically direct-deposits into your account every two weeks.

More predictability: Amazon won't suddenly yank your product (in most cases) or tell you today that you need to come up with ten times the inventory tomorrow because they want it in every store. Retail does that sort of thing.

More profitability, depending on your product: For a lightweight product that costs at least $30, your fees can be less than 25 percent. You typically have to give retail stores half of your take.

"Subscribe & Save": As long as you prove you can keep your product in stock in Amazon's warehouses, you're likely to be eligible for this program of theirs. From a stickiness standpoint, it's beautiful because when customers subscribe, you're set. You don't have to keep attracting the same people and hope that they pick you again next time; they're your subscribers now. You're selling more units than the number of people coming to the page that displays your product. It's great to know you have that baked-in revenue from subscribers, and you can see your subscription reports to understand what's already ordered for the next month.

A lot of feedback: When you sell in retail outlets, you don't know how people feel about your products. Well, some retailers do have reviews, as do direct-to-consumer sites, but most pale in comparison to the number on Amazon. You can chalk up that number to more than sales volume: Amazon also makes it easy to leave a review. The customer gets the email, clicks on stars, writes a few sentences, and boom! You get a clear picture of what customers like and don't like, so you can constantly improve what you offer.

A reliable technology: You don't have to worry about broken checkout or a slow or dropped page because Amazon has tens of thousands of developers worrying about it for you every minute of every day. It's a stable platform that you don't have to maintain. That's not to say Amazon has never crashed—think Prime Day, July 2018—but it's rare.

Handled shipping: If you spring for Prime, Amazon handles the shipping. The customer automatically gets the tracking number and can watch the whole cycle, and you don't hear those customers demanding, "Where's my stuff?!" If the product doesn't arrive, Amazon takes responsibility and makes it right with the customer.

Storefronts: Amazon has taken a page, so to speak, from platforms like Shopify, BigCommerce, and other eCommerce platforms. They are launching more ways to help you showcase your brand and all of your products in one place, upload videos, and tell your story. The storefronts look like mini websites within the Amazon site. (If you want to see an example, take a look at Prana clothing's brand page.)

Brand protection: In years past, anybody could post a listing for your product, it could look any way they wanted, and you'd have to fight to get Amazon to fix it, especially if you sold less than the lister. Now, when you use Amazon Brand Registry (and have a registered trademark), you have more authority over what pages containing your brand look like.

THE CONS

If I were to end this chapter with just the pros, you would think, "Looks great. Why shouldn't everybody sell on Amazon?" The answer is that there are downsides too. Most of them come down to "their sandbox, their rules," which are constantly changing, and some of them don't make sense.

Rule changes: New policies come up all the time that may not have anything to do with an individual brand but that cause it to scramble to try to comply. For example, in early 2018, the EPA sued Amazon for violating the Federal Insecticide, Fungicide, and Rodenticide Act because of some products stored in their warehouses and sold on the website. In addition to paying a fine, Amazon agreed to provide mandatory compliance training for brands that worked with them. As a result of the lawsuit, a lot of products sold on Amazon were considered in violation and suspended—so not available for purchase. Many people lost millions of dollars in sales.

Those people included a client of ours who sells an underwear product because you could no longer use the word "antibacterial." It's sort of hilarious to link a pair of underwear with a pesticide, but Amazon uses AI to scan everything, and the brand did have the forbidden word in the listing.

The same happens with food supplement brands. When Amazon deems an ingredient unsafe, they won't sell any brand that contains it.

Once your product is flagged, you're guilty and shut down until proven innocent. So you're always sort of sleeping with one foot on the ground, ready to jump up and respond when Amazon drops or suspends your listing for no reason.

The pesticide lawsuit affected about 25 percent of our clients, and they all had to go through the "seller performance" team to get their listings back up, but not before losing up to $10,000 a day for as many as seven days while they removed pesticide claims and got the page approved.

Big cut: There are three ways to sell on Amazon. One, is "sold and shipped by Amazon." You sell your products directly to Amazon and they pay you for them but not as much. That model is a lot like storefront retail where you have to give up 50 percent of the customer price while also paying for marketing and advertising.

By the time you're all done, you're lucky if you're left with 10 percent. If this method interests you (for some reason), you can't just send off your products. Amazon has to invite you.

The other ways to sell on Amazon are more democratic. Anyone can sign up, prove they're a legal business, and start selling. The second way is how most of our clients work, which is "shipped by Amazon, sold by you." Here you pay just two fees: a referral fee that varies by product category (8 percent on low-price grocery items to 17 percent on clothing) and an FBA (Fulfilled by Amazon) fee that includes Prime shipping. Their rates are better than the average consumer brand can get. They fulfill it for you, but you control the price, and you get paid when products sell.

The third way to sell through Amazon is "shipped and sold by you." In this case, you pay only the referral fee, and you ship to the customer. If your product is heavy and it doesn't cost much, it might cost too much to first pay to ship it to Amazon and then pay them to ship to the customer. If the product is one that customers don't mind waiting for, you might be better off sending it yourself by first-class mail.

For example, take an $80 baby activity gym that weighs about fourteen pounds. The FBA fee for something of that weight is about $24 on top of the 15 percent—or $12—referral fee. If you can ship it for less than that and the customer is patient, you probably want to do it.

If you're selling something in a business with a high rate of repeat sales, you're better off if you can keep the revenue yourself. That's also true if you're a brand that people are looking for, such as a popular clothing brand like Lululemon, rather than a commodity like batteries. But let's say your company makes workout tights, but you're not well known yet. In that case, Amazon could help you with product discovery because people are more likely to meet you when they do an unbranded search for that product.

And Prime Shipping helps build trust. I will not buy a product that ships from a seller because of the trust issue. If Amazon does the fulfillment, I know they are reputable and will treat me well if there are any shipping issues. The same can't be said for a product shipping from a company like DEALZ, DEALZ, DEALZ.

Sleep supplements is another example of a product that can get seen on Amazon without their makers going to the expense of paid search and paid social. Because thousands of people are searching for sleep aids without specifying a brand on Amazon, you've got a good shot at discovery.

Sell the product through an email campaign on your website, and you won't give up as much as 25 percent in fees to Amazon along with ownership of the customer. If it's a cheaper product, like batteries, or one that customers are likely to buy just once, that's a better fit for going through Amazon.

Extreme competition: Amazon punishes people who sell products for lower prices on their own websites or anywhere else. They make it harder for customers to buy what's "available from other sellers" by requiring extra clicks and removing their prices and Prime status from view.

Even worse news is that Amazon prevents your pay-per-click advertising from running, so it'll send your products into a downward spiral: most people will stop buying them, which will bump them from page one of the search results, making the products even less likely to sell. Amazon reports that 70 percent of their customers don't make it past that first results page.

So you're really stuck. Amazon is telling you to lower your

price, and if you don't, you'll live to regret it. But good luck getting the price raised on websites you don't control. If Target or one of your other partners runs a sale that includes your products, there's nothing you can do about it, and it's going to hurt you.

By the way, like paid search, Amazon's AI algorithm also looks to sales history to determine which products get page-one status. Typically, nothing with a 10 percent or lower conversion rate makes it, unless there are very few products for that search. That's a downside only if your products aren't appealing enough to sell. If they have a low conversion rate, let that stat be a word to the wise to improve your product's appeal.

Amazon's AI can work against you in other ways: During the summer months, you can't sell anything through Amazon's warehouses that can't tolerate 105 degrees. You have to actually remove anything that can melt, like a chocolate bar, and fulfill it yourself. A nutrition bar company we worked with yanked their meltable products out of the warehouses. But they thought they were safe with bars containing carob chips that passed a definitive heat test. Too bad it was automation making the call. AI didn't care about the test; it just turned off the listings.

You don't own the customer: Besides responding to a blind email question a customer might send about the product, you can't even talk to them, let alone own them. You're messaging through Amazon, so you don't get the value of their email address. You can't develop a relationship. If you're doing the shipping, you get the mailing address, but if you market to that address and Amazon finds out, they'll suspend your account.

I don't condone any violation of Amazon's terms of service, but some sellers try to get around the restrictions by slipping marketing inserts with barcodes into the box with the customer's order. The insert will usually carry a code and encourage the customer to scan it to receive a free product.

You can't even email people who write you a great review; you can only leave a comment and ask them to message you.

The lack of ownership in particular (along with less ability to build an exclusive brand and giving away up to 40 percent in margin) is why I advise any brand that built itself and sells only on their website, and maybe in their own stores, to resist the siren call of Amazon. They don't need to be there, and for them, the downsides outweigh the upsides of a little more revenue.

Favoring the customer over the seller: If there's ever a dispute between the seller and the customer (maybe the customer denies receiving the product that the seller can prove they sent), Amazon tends to err on the side of the customer.

Products now, payment later: Getting paid every two weeks is great, but that's for inventory you sent and that sat in Amazon's warehouses until it sold. When most brick-and-mortar retailers buy from you, on the other hand, they pay you upfront or a month or two after you send it. But they expect to pay whether it sells or not. The key to a good cash position with Amazon is maintaining the right amount of inventory at all times, so there's always cash coming in to pay for new products.

Bad actors, fake reviews: Some sellers on Amazon are writing their own reviews or getting people to do it for them in exchange for free products or actual payment. These come in all varieties: they'll slam their competitors' products, and praise to the sky their own products. We'll often see a competitive-product launch, and two weeks later, they'll have five-hundred too-good-to-be-true reviews, and you know that's not legitimate.

Amazon is continually cracking down on this. They've removed thousands of reviews, and they display a "Verified Purchase" label where it applies. That has been helpful. Amazon also gives more weight to more recent purchases because products tend to change. But they haven't been able to stop all the fakes. Unless there's actually profanity involved, it can be tough, particularly for AI, to tell the fakes from the real ones.

NUMBERS TO CONSIDER

So should you sell through Amazon or shouldn't you? I've given you a lot to think about.

If your decision comes down to money, as most decisions do, your next task is to run it through these numbers: each product's manufacturing cost, Amazon's fees, the cost to ship the product to Amazon, and advertising cost (which factors in the lifetime customer value and customer-acquisition cost, both mentioned in Chapter 4). Add 5 percent for miscellaneous expenses.

Total up your expenses and subtract them from your product price. If you can make at least 30 percent on Amazon, you're still better off than with retail stores.

HOW TO MAKE MORE OF THE MOST OF AMAZON

We've already talked about optimizing your product for price (finding the most profitable quantity). Keep looking at what you're offering and whether there's anything you can do to increase profitability. Also make sure you're on top of your costs to advertise on Amazon because the platform, like Google, is not in business to look out for you.

You also need to optimize your listing. Don't expect to get your sales on Amazon right until your product page works as well as it can. By product page, I mean both what customers can see—the product's title, bullets, images, and content—and the backend fields they can't see. If you fill out those fields correctly, you'll help your products show up higher in Amazon's search results.

One of those backend fields is for keyword. Let's say your company makes a hazelnut spread, and that's exactly what most people search for to find it. A few customers, though, search for "filbert," another word for hazelnut. They are so few that you might not want that word to show up anywhere on the page because your branding is all about the hazelnut. But you can put the other word in the backend keyword field and cover your bases.

Every single company that has come to us for help has had a suboptimal listing. When we show them how to optimize their title, their bullets, and their images, their conversion rate increases.

For example, an additional skincare brand came to us with only a 15 percent conversion rate. When we ran our playbook on their listing, they doubled both their conversion rate and their revenue.

KNOWLEDGE IS PROFIT

The natural cleaning products brand that began this chapter was a textbook example of the risks of selling on Amazon without knowing the ropes. As soon as we removed the wrong products and reconfigured the right ones, the company's Amazon revenue began to take off.

Amazon can provide a significant part of your revenue if you're selling a commodity *and* you understand how to make it pay for you and how to play nicely in their sandbox. You understand those things now, so you're way ahead of all the people who've lost money on Amazon because they didn't know what they were doing. You know not only the answer to "Should I sell on Amazon?" but, if it's yes, also the answer to "How should I sell there?"

Do...

...figure out how much Amazon will take in fees before you start the journey to sell on that platform. Make sure you can be profitable.

...make sure you have a registered and live trademark with the US Patent and Trademark office. If you don't, start the process now because approval can take up to nine months.

...follow Amazon's rules and policies. As much as you may not agree with them, complying will keep you in good standing with the marketplace.

Absolutely Don't...

...live with a less-than-perfect product page, including great images, titles, description, and backend fields—at the very least. Amazon judges and ranks products by their popularity in their first thirty days after launch.

...try to "fight" with Amazon. They err on the side of the customer, not the seller.

So now it's time to wrap this thing up now and send you off to make your fortune online.

Conclusion

You've just traveled through a wealth of knowledge I've gained over the past twenty years helping companies build profitable online businesses. I'm hoping that the successes and failures I've shared will help you reach success a lot more quickly and skip the failure part.

The examples and advice come down to this: If your business isn't moving forward, or moving at the rate you expect, there's so much you can do to turn it around. That starts with taking a clear, hard look at your business, its foundation, and its numbers, and it ends with making—or unmaking—your every decision based on them.

Let's review your journey through this book.

CORE VALUES

If you can get your core values right, it creates an amazing culture where everyone is aligned around the same things. A company culture based on core values gets you team members who go out of their way to constantly improve the experience for your customers, and by extension, the size of your revenue.

HIRING AND FIRING

People are expensive to hire, to train, and, if things don't work out, to fire. Make sure that every person on your ship embraces your core values and believes it's not only possible but worthwhile to share your company's goals and help you reach them.

CUSTOMER SERVICE THAT CREATES CUSTOMER ADVOCATES

Treat your customers like the precious entities they are.

Find out what would thrill them, make it happen, and they'll reward you with loyalty. They'll express that loyalty in repeat sales and delighted reviews on social media, which turn into a lot more customers on the repeat-sales cycle.

HOW TO BE PROFITABLE

You can't stay in business if you're not profitable, so it's worth your time to understand your numbers and profitability and explore how to boost them. Maybe it's shifting your cash cycle, reducing your product costs, finding more affordable ways to find customers, or the many other strategies you read about in Chapter 4.

DIRECT-TO-CONSUMER ONLINE SALES

I love direct-to-consumer selling online for certain types of products. Its many benefits over storefront retail and Amazon include the abilities to form a relationship with your customers and to control both your brand presentation and your product prices.

AMAZON SALES

Amazon can be either great for your business or awful for it, depending on your business, your products, and your costs. If it makes sense for you to sell there and you do it right, it can drive a significant portion of your revenue.

Now that you've finished the book, I'm giving you plenty of homework.

ASSIGNMENT #1: EVALUATE

Before you do anything else, evaluate your business from the standpoint of everything you've learned here. Take a day away from your office to get a clear perspective on your business foundations and numbers.

ASSIGNMENT #2: LIST YOUR STEPS

List your next steps to determine what you can do and in what order to make the most impact. You can fill out a quadrant matrix like the one below.

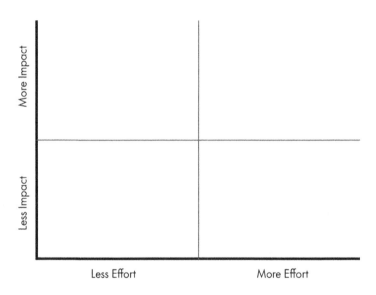

ASSIGNMENT #3: NETWORK

Have as many conversations as you can with people whose

businesses you admire. Identify brands that complement yours, meaning that they're not competitive with you and that, like your business, don't seem to have unlimited resources. Share, ask, and learn: "What are your core values?" "How do you do paid search?" "What about paid social?" "What has worked for you in email marketing?"

You can also join a CEO, mastermind, or social media group and have opportunities to share and learn with a number of people at once. As a member of BEAM Angel Network, I mentor women who are new founders.

ASSIGNMENT #4: HIRE THE RIGHT AGENCY

Before you put your trust in any agency, including ours, ask these six questions to gauge whether they're worth your time and money and whether you can hold them accountable:

1. "What's the ROAS (return on ad spend) of your clients who've been with you at least two months?" Ask for a printout with redacted names. At least 80 percent of their clients should be getting at least $2 for every dollar spent.
2. "Can you give me client references?"
3. "Can I own my ad account?" Make sure that you set up the Google or Facebook account for your brand on your own, and then give access to the agency. If they set it

up instead and you leave, you've lost all your historical data.

4. "How long will it take me to scale?" You should see progress within two months. Tell them your goal, how long they expect it to take, and what they intend to do if they don't help you reach it.

5. "Do you have a guarantee?" We do; we refund half the fees paid to us after two months if people aren't satisfied, and we've had to do that only once in our four years in business. That was for a client we should not have accepted in the first place because they didn't fit our typical client description.

6. "What should my key performance indicators be?"

AT YOUR SERVICE

If you find you can use help with any of this, call me. You'll find my contact and more information on our agency's website, roiswift.com. I wish you every success in your business, and I sincerely hope I've helped you reach it.

About the Author

CAROLYN (BYRON) LOWE is the founder and CEO of ROI Swift, a digital marketing agency based in Austin, Texas. Over the last twenty years, from the early days of Dell Consumer Marketing to the current digital age when people are Instacarting dog food, Carolyn has been at the forefront of consumer online marketing and acquisition. She has helped to profitably grow all types of companies, from *Fortune 500*s to two-person startups.

Carolyn derives great pleasure from seeing emerging brands grow, realize their dreams, and be successful, thus her goal: to grow a thousand emerging brands by 2030. She and her team at ROI Swift have eight hundred to go until she retires. That's some job security.

Carolyn won $10,000 on the radio when she was fourteen

and wishes she had saved it to invest in Amazon or Google in early 2000. Carolyn, a licensed pilot with no time to fly these days, lives with her husband and their two children in Austin, Texas.

Made in the USA
Monee, IL
23 September 2021